797,885 Books
are available to read at

Forgotten Books

www.ForgottenBooks.com

Forgotten Books' App
Available for mobile, tablet & eReader

ISBN 978-1-333-45840-9
PIBN 10507098

This book is a reproduction of an important historical work. Forgotten Books uses state-of-the-art technology to digitally reconstruct the work, preserving the original format whilst repairing imperfections present in the aged copy. In rare cases, an imperfection in the original, such as a blemish or missing page, may be replicated in our edition. We do, however, repair the vast majority of imperfections successfully; any imperfections that remain are intentionally left to preserve the state of such historical works.

Forgotten Books is a registered trademark of FB &c Ltd.
Copyright © 2015 FB &c Ltd.
FB &c Ltd, Dalton House, 60 Windsor Avenue, London, SW19 2RR.
Company number 08720141. Registered in England and Wales.

For support please visit www.forgottenbooks.com

1 MONTH OF FREE READING

at

www.ForgottenBooks.com

By purchasing this book you are eligible for one month membership to ForgottenBooks.com, giving you unlimited access to our entire collection of over 700,000 titles via our web site and mobile apps.

To claim your free month visit:
www.forgottenbooks.com/free507098

* Offer is valid for 45 days from date of purchase. Terms and conditions apply.

English
Français
Deutsche
Italiano
Español
Português

www.forgottenbooks.com

Mythology Photography **Fiction**
Fishing Christianity **Art** Cooking
Essays Buddhism Freemasonry
Medicine **Biology** Music **Ancient Egypt** Evolution Carpentry Physics
Dance Geology **Mathematics** Fitness
Shakespeare **Folklore** Yoga Marketing
Confidence Immortality Biographies
Poetry **Psychology** Witchcraft
Electronics Chemistry History **Law**
Accounting **Philosophy** Anthropology
Alchemy Drama Quantum Mechanics
Atheism Sexual Health **Ancient History**
Entrepreneurship Languages Sport
Paleontology Needlework Islam
Metaphysics Investment Archaeology
Parenting Statistics Criminology
Motivational

THE LITTLE BAPTIST

THE

LITTLE BAPTIST:

BY
J. M. MARTIN.

"And that from a child thou hast known the holy scriptures, which are able to make thee wise unto salvation through faith which is in Christ Jesus."
2 Timothy 3:15

LOUISVILLE, KY.
BAPTIST BOOK CONCERN,
1848.

PUBLISHERS PREFACE

We send forth "THE LITTLE BAPTIST", with a prayer that the reader may be stirred by the clarity and sincerity of thought and understanding, which this work reveals concerning the great Baptist Distinctives, that we hold so dear.

"THE LITTLE BAPTIST", is written so that a child or an adult may read it with equal enjoyment and learning.

"THE LITTLE BAPTIST", has been out of print since 1848. It was written by J. M. Martin of Rienzi, Mississippi, and was published by the Baptist Book Concern well before the Civil War.

NOTE: This work is in its original format and has not been changed.

Printed By:
Fargo Baptist Church
Fargo, ND

Bound, Published, and
Distributed By:
Parker Memorial Baptist Church
1902 E. Cavanuagh Rd.
Lansing, MI 48910
(517) 882-2112

PREFACE

I have written a book; not for the student of classic lore, but for the young, to whom plain truths are of more value than polished style. Should it serve the cause of truth, I shall be content for critics to exercise their talents upon its imperfections. The object of the book is to give a plain, common sense view of the doctrines of the gospel, and to present, in a simple style, the peculiar features distinguishing Baptists from all other Christian denominations I have no design against the Presbyterians. as such, but select them only as representatives of the great Pedo-baptist family. The expressions that Dr. Farnsworth is made to use, are generally the stereotyped sentences used by Methodist and Presbyterian controversialists with whom I am acquainted. The trial and expulsion of Mrs. Brown from the church, is introduced merely to form a basis from which to present the Communion question in its true light, and not with a view to show intolerance in the Presbyterian church.

With whatever imperfections the book may have, and with a just feeling of responsibility for the result of its teachings, I send it forth, attended by a fervent prayer that it may be instrumental in the accomplishment of much good.

I. M. MARTIN.
Rienzi, Miss.

PREFACE TO NEW EDITION.

When the plates of this wonderful book became so worn by the issue of over 100,000 copies that the making of new plates was necessary, it was deemed best to have the book carefully edited. I have, therefore, gone over it and have eliminated some defects and some superfluities of expression, but in no case has the sense been changed. The aim has been to make it plainer.

I have added the statement of the offer of $1,000 reward for the production of a single passage in the Greek of either the classic or the New Testament period where baptizo means sprinkle or pour, and have given some testimonies of leading scholars of different denominations.

It is confidently hoped that this great little book, whose author builded even better than he knew, will enter upon a greater sphere of usefulness than ever. It has already led its thousands to New Testament truth and practice,—may it continue to lead its tens of thousands.

T. T. EATON.

Louisville, Ky.

THE LITTLE BAPTIST.

CHAPTER I.

THE SURPRISE.

"O MAMMA! look here! This Bible that brother gave me, is a *Baptist* Bible. I am sure that brother didn't know it, else he would not have given it to me; and I *won't have it*. The merchant cheated him; don't you think he did, mamma?"

"Why, darling, what have you found in it to make you talk so? Don't you know that your brother bought you the best Bible he could find, and are you not going to be satisfied with it?"

'No, mamma, because it's a Baptist Bible—*I know it is*; and I don't want a Baptist Bible. I do wish Buddie hadn't gone to college, so I could have him take it back and get me one of the right kind. 0, it is such a nice book, I am so sorry there is a mistake about it. *I do wish it was right.*"

"Yes, but it is right, dear; I don't understand your crazy notion. Yours is like your brother's Bible that he carried away with him; just like the large family Bible from which I have often read to you; the reading in all of them is just the same."

"But, mamma, mine is a Baptist Bible; *it is in fact*. It tells so plainly about baptizing people *in rivers*, and places where there was *much water*, and about *going down into* the water, and coming *up out of* the water, just for all the world like Mr. Coleman, the Baptist preacher, baptizes people. And surely, if the big Bible reads that way, you would not have had Dr. Farnsworth to sprinkle a little water on my face, and to just wet his fingers and rub them on little sister's face, and call it *baptism*. And, mamma, if the big Bible does read that way, why did you always skip those places when you were reading to me?"

"O, fie, child! you ask more questions in a minute than I could answer in a day; but there is one thing you may understand, that is, that the Baptists, the Methodists and *our church*, as well as all other Protestant churches, have the same kind of Bibles."

"Why, mamma, they don't all do alike, yet don't they all say they believe the Bible? I can't see how it is, unless their Bibles are wrong."

"No, my dear, the difference is in the way different people understand the Bible. The Baptists understand it to teach some things just the reverse of what Presbyterians and others do; but this only amounts to an honest difference of opinion."

"Well, but mamma, is not Dr. Flarnsworth as smart as the Baptist preacher? Mr. Coleman talks just like my Bible reads, and if he can understand it, why can't Dr. Farnsworth understand it, too?"

THE LITTLE BAPTIST.

The speaker was little Mellie Brown, with rosy cheeks and flaxen hair, who had just passed her tenth birthday, on which her brother Frank had given her a very fine little pocket Bible. At the time of the conversation she was sitting in her little rocking chair at her mother's side, reading the third chapter of Matthew; and when she read the account of John the Baptist baptizing the people in the Jordan, she was persuaded that the bookseller had practiced a fraud on her brother, by selling him a Baptist Bible. Such a thought as evading a plain declaration of Scripture, had never entered her mind. But in her child-like simplicity, she had supposed the Bible to mean what it said, and to say what it meant. And she had received the impression that the Baptists were in error, regarding the action of baptism, which very readily explains her great surprise when she began to read the Bible for herself.

Mellie had been taught that the Bible was the Word of God, and that all its teachings should be obeyed. Her mother had taken much pains to cultivate her mind, and took pride in witnessing the unfolding of her genius. She was so remarkable for intelligence and sober thought, that she attracted special attention, and became the general favorite among her acquaintances. Books were her chief delight, and whenever she got a new one, she was devoted to it, until she had read it through. So her new Bible became her constant companion. She had a great desire to know the meaning of all that she read and spent much of her time in asking questions of her mother and others, touching what she had been reading.

CHAPTER II.

THE PARENTS.

COLONEL BROWN had been reared in the Presbyterian church; but when he settled in the town of H——, in Mississippi, he claimed no church relation, and was entirely a "man of the world." He was an upright and honorable man, of excellent morals, kind, affable and social in his intercourse with others. His noble and generous traits of character had gained him a large popularity, and he seldom failed to be chosen to some important official position. In regard to religion, he became a *Liberalist*, conceding orthodoxy to all creeds, and catholicity to all sects. To experimental Christianity he was wholly a stranger, and was a living monument to the fact that being baptized in infancy, and growing up in the church, give no guarantee of an inward work of grace. Col. Brown lacked the "one thing needful"—true piety—and knowing not the power of godliness, he had discarded its forms, and held himself aloof from his church.

Mrs. Brown was very different. Though of almost opposite temperaments, they lived together with but little discord, and well illustrated the possibility of "harmonious differences." She had reserved humility, patience and kindness, that commended her as the model wife, the exemplary Christian, affectionate mother, and kind neighbor. She knew the power of experimental religion, and in her intercourse with the world, although herself one of the brightest ornaments of society, she sought not for honor, but was governed by her sense of duty. She did not inquire "What can I do?" but "What ought I to do?" and wherever duty pointed the way she did not hesitate to follow. She was devoted to her church, and her heart and hands were open to the poor. In her, meekness, courage, and humility were beautifully blended; and her Christian influence was felt throughout the circle of her acquaintance.

Mrs. Brown was not reared in the church, but under the influence of Presbyterianism; so when she married into a Presbyterian family, and professed religion, she very naturally united with that church. Notwithstanding, her mind was superior, and her education liberal, she had one failing that was inexcusable. Like thousands of others, she let other people do her thinking in religious matters. In regard to doctrines, ordinances, and church polity, especially, she accepted the conclusions of others, without taking the pains to investigate for herself. Instead of giving personal attention to these things, it was enough for her to know that the church endorsed a doctrine or a practice. Her faith was in her church. The decisions of her church satisfied both her mind and her conscience. Or, rather, it satisfied her judgment, for as matter of course, the conscience approves whatever the judgment pronounces right. Although she could see no reason for controversy on the subject of baptism, and, in candor, could but admit that the Bible was silent in reference to any other than believer's baptism, and decidedly plain as to the action having been immersion in apostolic times, yet, she would say, "Others of more extensive learning and research have agreed that sprinkling and pouring are of equal validity with immersion, and that infants are duly entitled to baptism, too, and I suppose they have good reasons for thinking so, else, as honest people, they would not teach and practice as they do." Thus she "pinned her faith to the sleeves" of other people, and quietly floated on with the current of her church, giving the subject but little serious attention, thinking that so many persons of exalted piety and wisdom could not be deceived. And, since so many good people had gone to Heaven with no other baptism than that which her church administered, it would be sufficient for herself also.

When her little daughter expressed such surprise on discovering what she supposed to be a Baptist Bible, she was no less astonished than amused, but as she reflected the subject assumed a more serious aspect. Said she, "If the Bible is so plain upon this subject that even a child can understand it at a glance, I may be guilty of gross neglect."

It was hard for her to consent that her church was in error, and she resolved that none but the most positive testimony should convince her of it. A thought had been awakened, however and though she resolved only to think silently herself, she would be no hindrance to an impartial investigation of the Bible by her child. She felt anxious to see what conclusion an unprejudiced mind would reach, exempt from all other influence than the Bible. Like other fond mothers she doted on her child. She knew her intellect was more than ordinary, and she desired to see that intellect thoroughly cultivated; hence she determined to aid her in making improvement in every way possible.

CHAPTER III.

CONVERSATION ABOUT THE BIBLE.

MELLIE became satisfied that there was no mistake about her Bible, and continued to read it, and to ask her mother the meaning of texts which she did not fully understand. Mrs. Brown took great pains to explain to Mellie all about the Bible. How it was first written by men inspired of God; but that it was not first given in our language, therefore had been translated from other languages into the English. That a good and wise king of England, named James, seeing the great need among the people of the Bible in a language that they could read, employed a number of the best scholars in his kingdom, and had them to translate it into the English language. "And this translation," said she, "is the Bible that we now have."

"But, mamma, everybody don't use it, do they?" asked Mellie with an air of sober reflection.

"Yes," continued Mrs. Brown; "those who speak the English language, except the Roman Catholics; they have a translation differing in some respects from this, but the Episcopalians, Methodists, Baptists and Presbyterians, with other sects in our country, all take this as the Word of God."

Mellie pushed back her hair, gave her chair a

hitch up closer to her mother, and replied:

"It's very strange that they don't all agree then, if God tells them all the same things. I think God won't like those much who will not do what He tells them. But mamma, what do you mean by *translating* the Bible?"

"To translate, my dear, is to change the words which are in one language into the words of another with the same meaning. Words, you know, are signs of ideas, and we get the idea, or meaning, of the words in one language, and express it by using the words of another language."

Mrs. Brown further explained that the writers of the Old Testament wrote in the Hebrew language, and the writers of the New Testament in the Greek language, and in order to give us their meaning, scholars who understood these languages had given the ideas to us in words of which we know the meaning.

"Yes, mamma," said Mellie, "I think that I understand you, and I think it was very kind in King James to have the Bible translated into a language that the people can read and understand. But you have always told me that it is the Book of God, and if the people all think that it is His book, I can't see why they don't all read it, and do just what it tells them. Now you know, mamma, that Dr. Farnsworth preached last Sunday that people were God's children, or I thought that was what he meant; and he said they ought to look to God to learn their duty, and when God tells them in the Bible what they must do, they ought to do it willingly, just like a good child obeying its parents. You know, mamma, that you always praise me, and call me your little darling when I do as you tell me, and you say if I disobey you will have to punish me for it. Then, if people are God's children, I think they ought to read His book, and then do whatever it tells them. Don't you think so, mamma?"

"Yes, dear; but you know that bad people, like bad children, do not care to do what is right. They rather take pleasure in doing evil. But all good people want to do right—they want to do just as God tells them."

"But the *good* people don't all do alike, mamma. You said that Mr. Coleman, the Baptist preacher, was a good man, and I know Dr. Farnsworth is a good man; but they don't both do alike—I know they don't. They both have God's book to tell them how to do, and yet when Dr. Farnsworth baptizes people, he just takes a *little* water in his hand and wets a little place on their heads, and Mr. Coleman leads them down into deep water, and puts them all over into it. And I think that John the Baptist must"—

Mellie was going on to say that she thought John the Baptist must have put the people all over in the water, too; but her mother stopped her by saying that it was a difference in understanding the Bible that caused the different denominations to practice differently; "And," said she, "I have no doubt but that all honestly think they are right. I believe that Dr. Farnsworth, and Mr. Coleman, both have honest intentions, and are trying to obey God as best they can. They can't both see alike in reference to baptism, and, therefore, they don't do alike."

"Well, mamma, I'm going to read my little Bible and I'm going to be good, and do all it says for me to do. I intend to see how much of it I can understand, and if there is any of it that God has not made plain so people can understand it, I guess it is about something that He don't want us to do. I'll see what it says about baptizing folks and everything else. God wants us to read His Bible, don't He, mamma?"

"True, my child, and I'm glad to find you so determined to read and be good. When you find anything that you can't understand, come to me and I will try to explain it to you. I want you to see how much you can learn. Should we find anything in reading that is too hard for us, we will ask Dr. Farnsworth to explain it when he calls, and you shall understand all that your Bible teaches. It is only a month now until you will start to school. Then I hope you will learn a great deal about the Bible as well as your other books."

"And I shall be so glad to go to school, mamma, for then I will *have such a nice time.* I'll ask Mr. Hamilton to let me study Grammar and History—yes, and Botany, so I can go in the class with Laura Thompson, Nellie Perkins, Katie Jones and all the larger girls. I intend to try to beat them all, too, I don't care if they are older than I am; I'll make them work for it, if they keep ahead of me. O, I do wish school was open now."

Saying this she bounded from the room perfectly elated with the thought of going to school.

CHAPTER IV.

MELLIE AT SCHOOL.

WHEN the morning came for Mr. Hamilton to open his school, Mellie Brown was there at an early hour, with her satchel of books, eager to begin her lessons. After a short examination, Mr. Hamilton permitted her to enter the class of her choice. She was found to be equal to many who were much her senior, and who had spent much more time at school.

Mellie soon became a great favorite in the school, and especially so of her teacher. Mr. Hamilton was not long in discovering her rare mental capacity, and in appreciating her genial and lovely disposition. And it is not at all strange that he conceived for her a feeling of partiality; not that he let this make any difference in his treatment of her and the others, but, with superior merit on her side, he gave her extra attention, yet with no design of invidious discriminations. Mellie was highly attractive: small for her age, a beautiful face, a bright countenance, her every look and action revealing a mild and pleasant temperament.

In her deportment, she was systematic and orderly. At her studies she was expert and energetic. No bad marks were ever given her for misconduct; but when a prize was offered in her class, she was generally the fortunate contestant, because she never failed to *try*, and always *did her best*. Often she might be heard singing:

"If you find your task is hard—Try, try again;
Time will bring you your reward—Try, try again;
All that other folks can do,
Why with patience may not you?
Only keep this rule in view, Try, try again."

An intimacy soon grew up between her and her teacher, so that she felt no hesitancy in asking him questions. Often her questions were touching some person or doctrine in the Bible. She always carried her Bible with her, and daily read it as circumstances would admit; and when alone she would mark texts to have explained by her mother or teacher at some convenient time.

Mr. Hamilton frequently required his school to read a chapter in the Bible as a part of the morning exercises, and it was not at all unusual for Mellie to interrupt the reading by some impromptu question, which it seemed she could not restrain. This practice, though not in accord with strict propriety, was tolerated in her because of her simplicity and honesty of purpose, as well as the kind, ingenious and confiding manner in which she would ask the questions. The teacher often answered in a way to profit all the school, and imparted much useful information to his pupils that he never would have done but for the inquisitive, *thinking* little Mellie Brown.

One morning the New Testament lesson was

the eighth chapter of the Acts of the Apostles, and it happened to come Mellie's time to read the thirty-eighth verse, which describes the scene of Philip going down into the water to baptize the eunuch. She finished the verse and stood in deep reflection while the next in the class read: "And when they were come up out of the water," etc. Mellie, as if moved by some irresistible emotion, put a stop to the reading by saying: "Mr. Hamilton, Philip was a Baptist, wasn't he?"

Taken by surprise, Mr. Hamilton was confused for a time, but reflecting a little he replied: "Well, it does look a little like he might have been, but why, Mellie do you wish to know that?"

"Because," said Mellie, "I just thought that he baptized the man like the Baptists baptize people, and I suppose he must have been a Baptist."

"I can't say about that," said Mr. Hamilton, "this is a subject of controversy in the churches, and as it is not my business to teach sectarianism, nor to have such topics discussed in my school, we will proceed at once with the lesson."

Mellie received many *cutting* winks and looks from the other pupils, and, of course, felt severely rebuked by the summary manner in which her question had been disposed of. Mr. Hamilton acted only from prudential reasons in bringing the matter to a hasty conclusion, yet he enjoyed the novelty of having the exercises of his school suspended for a discussion on the subject of baptism, and often referred to it as "a good joke" on his school. But to show the little questioner that he was not offended with her, he called her to him at recess, and said, "Come now, Mellie, if you are willing, we will talk some more about Philip's being a Baptist."

Mellie approached him with more than usual diffidence, but when she was assured that her motives were appreciated, and her little impropriety excused, she mustered courage to again ask Mr. Hamilton if he did not think that Philip baptized the man just like the Baptists baptize people, he evaded by saying:

"Why, Mellie, I thought you were a good little Presbyterian; are you about to turn Baptist? If you do, what will your Ma and Dr. Farnsworth say to it?"

"I don't know, Mr. Hamilton," said Mellie, "I never thought about being anything now, but when I get older and understand all about the Bible, I am going to do whatever it says. But it appears to me that the Bible is a Baptist book anyway, for almost every place that baptism is mentioned, it was in a river or at a place of much water, and it tells about the people going down into and coming up out of the water. That's the way my Bible reads, and mamma says that it is just like other Bibles. Buddie gave it to me, and when I read it, I thought there was some mistake about it: that some Baptist had printed it just to make Baptists of the people, because it reads so much like they preach and practice; but it is exactly like Laura Thompson's and Nannie Gordon's, and I guess it must be right. But Mr. Hamilton won't you tell me what you think?"

"No, Mellie, I don't teach school to influence

my pupils one way or the other about such questions as baptism. You can read your Bible and act according to its instructions, or else your parents and the preachers must teach you. I have no doubt that when you get older, you will be able to form satisfactory conclusions for yourself. I advise you to persevere in your investigations, and learn all that you can about the Bible, and I am sure that my little pet will be willing to do whatever her Bible teaches her is right."

"Yes, that I will; Buddie told me to read the Bible, and to do whatever it said do, and I'm going to stick to the lines I learned in my little primer when I was only five years old:

>'My book and heart,
>Shall never part;'

and if my little Bible does turn out to be a Baptist book, why, then, I'm going to be a little Baptist, *sure enough.*"

As it was near the time for school, Mr. Hamilton walked out for a little recreation, and the girls who had been listening to the conversation, began to ridicule Mellie for what they were pleased to call her "impertinence" and "presumption." Katy Jones exclaimed, "La, Mell, you going to be a Baptist, and your ma a Presbyterian! Why, what will folks think?"

"I know what I'll think," said Mellie, "I'll think it's nobody's business. If my Bible makes me a little Baptist, why then, I'll be a Baptist, and that's all of it. But let us get to our lessons before the teacher returns, just to show him how much we want to learn."

But Katy Jones and Laura Thompson began to tantalize her, and to call her, "The little Baptist;" and asked her if she hadn't better send back to Jerusalem and get Philip to come and baptize her, and a great many other things equally absurd; but the unexpected entrance of the teacher restored order, and a gentle tap of his bell summoned all to their lessons.

Mellie felt that it was very unkind in the girls to tease her so for her honest expressions, yet she did not weep or pout, as many girls would have done. She thought as little about it as possible, and when the time came for reciting her lesson, she was not behind any in the class. When she returned home in the evening, she spent a short time playing with her dolls. After re-arranging some of their dresses, and putting all in order, she placed them smugly in a little box for their night's rest. Then she must go and see that the little ducks and chickens were fed and housed for the night; and after she had asked her mother many questions about the affairs of the kitchen, garden and various interests, she was ready to take her little sister Anna out for an evening walk.

By the time these rounds were through, her mind was pretty well rested from the labors of the day, and she was then ready to apply herself to the lesson that she must recite the next morning. She had at this time an unusually hard lesson, and her mind not being altogether free from the conflicts of the day, it was late before she was sure that her lesson was prepared, and she was summoned to bed before she thought of putting by her books. When she went to kiss her mother "good-night," she said: "Mamma, I think the girls treated me very unkindly to-day; I would not have thought that they would have done so."

"Who, dear?"

"Why, Laura Thompson, and all the big girls; and all because I asked Mr. Hamilton something about the reading in the Bible."

And she gave an account of what had occurred over the New Testament lesson, and how the girls ridiculed her and called her "The little Baptist." but, said she, "I am not going to care for it, but will study hard and try to beat every one of them. I'll show them that if I am the least one in the class, I know how to do right; and I won't care for it."

Mrs. Brown, always proud of her daughter, felt flattered afresh by this additional evidence of Mellie's superiority. She spoke approvingly of her determination, and told her that the best way to treat mockers and tattlers was to live and act above the reach of their influence.

"But, mamma," said Mellie, "I think I have learned something from the Bible about the right way to treat the girls when they make fun of me. It teaches me to do good for evil."

"Yes," said Mrs. Brown, "and it says that you must forgive those that wrong you—or sin against you."

"Yes, it does, mamma; I've read it; and it says if we don't forgive those who trespass against us, our Heavenly Father will not forgive us. Then I'll forgive the girls, for you know I must do whatever my Bible tells me to do. That's right, isn't it, mamma?"

Mellie scarcely heard her mother's approving answer, for she had hardly finished the sentence until she was quietly sleeping, and did not awake until the light of another day came peeping in at her window. Rising quickly and dressing, she hurried out to release the ducks and chickens from the little prisons to which she had consigned them for the night; then she paid a visit to her box of dolls to see that no old rat had intruded on her interesting little family; next a romp over the house with little Anna and the kittens, and she was ready to go about preparing her toilet for breakfast. After breakfast her lesson must be reviewed, then she was off to school.

Arriving at the school-house, she found many of her class in advance of her, and this morning the teacher was unusually late. Mellie was greeted on all sides by the girls with "Good morning, little Baptist." "How do you do, little Baptist?" and, "I hope the little Baptist is well this morning;" to all of which she returned a pleasant "Good-morning," and walking to her desk, quietly deposited her books. She then said: "How have you all succeeded with that hard lesson? I suppose, though, you are all ready to recite, as you appear to be idle."

"We don't look for you to have a good lesson this morning, Mell," said Katy Jones, "for we know you have not studied it; you've been reading that Baptist Bible. But, of course, Mr. Hamilton will excuse you, *under the circumstances.*"

"Yes, *of course,*" said Laura Thompson, "Mr. Hamilton will excuse *her* for anything, as she's his *little pet.*" Turning to Nannie Gordon she said: "I do believe that Mr. Hamilton thinks that Mell is a little piece of perfection, and I shall not be surprised if he makes her an assistant teacher in the school before long. You can all *see* that whatever she does is exactly right; and then, *she knows it all*--all that is worth knowing."

"A pretty assistant teacher she would make," said Nelly Perkins; "now wouldn't she cut a figure explaining that Bible?"

"I rather guess," said Alice Green, "that she would be better on asking questions, than in giving explanations."

"Yes, the little inquisitive Miss," said Mellie Turner; "she is a very nice size for an interrogation point, and that's the use I'd put her to, if I were Mr. Hamilton. I would put her up somewhere in the house as a sign of inquisitiveness."

The teacher entered, and the young ladies were forced to retire from the attack, mortified, too, because they had failed to stir up resentment, or cause her to speak a single word in retaliation. The girls had exhibited a spirit that could only have been the offspring of envy and jealousy, which had been engendered because Mellie had outstripped them all in gaining the respect and attention of the teacher. Mellie felt that it was no fault of hers that her teacher had treated her with more attention than he had extended to others, therefore she disregarded their taunts and jeers, and went about her lessons with perfect self-possession.

Several days passed during which the girls tried every means to vex Mellie into resentment. Whenever they could catch her eye they would point their fingers, or make ugly mouths at her, or do something else to try to aggravate her. But all to no purpose. Sometimes she would say to them.

"Be you to others kind and true,
As you would have them be to you."

This with other kind replies, the sentiment, if not the language of which she had read in her Bible, gratified all the spirit of revenge she felt.

One day Laura Thompson tried to persuade Mellie to take Sallie Morgan's apples from her basket, when Mellie, with much surprise, exclaimed, "Laura! do you think that I would do such a thing as that? I know better than to steal apples. Do you think to make me believe that it would be no harm, when the Bible says, 'Thou shalt not steal?'"

"Pshaw," said Laura; "that's nothing, just to take a few apples—nobody will know it."

"God would know it," said Mellie, "and if He did not, I'd be ashamed to see myself do such a thing. I don't need Sallie Morgan's apples, but if

I did, I would go and ask her for them, like anybody ought to do."

CHAPTER V.

DOING GOOD FOR EVIL.

ONE morning Mr. Hamilton opened school by reading the twelfth chapter of Romans. During the reading Mollie marked several places she desired to have explained, but she preserved silence until the last verse was read: "Be not overcome of evil, but overcome evil with good," when she asked Mr. Hamilton to explain it, saying: "Mamma talked to me once about doing good for evil, and about forgiving persons who offended me; and I read in my Bible that God said, if we forgive not each other's trespasses, He will not forgive us when we sin against Him. I think this is the meaning of it, and I thought that this text might mean that by being good to others we could make them better."

Although reserved in giving opinions on any subject that might have sectarian bearing, in this instance Mr. Hamilton felt no such restraints. He was, indeed, glad of the opportunity of enforcing this text on the minds of his pupils. So after giving his sanction to Mellie's conclusions, he addressed the school as follows:

"We can have no stronger evidence of a firm and well founded Christian principle in a person than to see them capable of forgiving injuries and returning good for evil. The Saviour taught us to love our enemies; do good to them that hate us, and pray for them that despitefully use us, that we may be the children of our Father in Heaven, who maketh His sun to shine on the evil and good, and sendeth the rain on the just and on the unjust. He tells us to be perfect, even as our Father in Heaven is perfect. Paul tells us to let love be without dissimulation, that is without false pretension or hypocrisy; to abhor that which is evil and cleave to that which is good; to be kindly affectioned one toward another. Again, he says, bless them that persecute you: bless, and curse not, for vengeance is mine; I will repay, saith the Lord. Therefore we should never return evil for evil, but if our enemy hunger, we should feed him, and if he thirst, we should give him drink; for in so doing we heap coals of fire on his head. In this way we may overcome evil with good. Now, for instance, if any of the girls were to mistreat one of you by calling you ill names, or otherwise abuse you, and you were to get angry and treat them in the same way, that would not be like our Heavenly Father treats those who sin against Him. He ever remains kind to all, and His mercy is over all continually. But if, when you are mistreated, you render kindness in return, and show that you are above doing so low a thing as to treat them in like manner, still manifesting a kind regard for them, you thereby disarm them of malice, and conquer their evil dispositions. This is about what the apostle means by 'heaping coals of fire on their heads."

"O, yes, I see now," said Mellie, "how that is; I thought he could not mean putting burning coals on them, because that might make them angry again. I think now that I can understand it all. It's when one does another a great wrong, and gets kind treatment in return, it makes that person so ashamed and so sorry that the suffer-ings of the heart are as burning coals of fire on the head. O, I do wish I could understand all that the Bible means, and I intend to keep trying. I'll read it carefully, and I'll get you and mamma to tell me what I can't understand and when I get larger I will know more about it."

The conversation now had to give way to other duties, but as they repaired to their lessons, a marked difference was manifest in the countenances of the pupils. Mellie's cheerful spirit shone out through her eyes, and lit up her whole countenance with almost angelic brightness. She felt that she had done her duty, and her conscience was at ease. But with Laura Thompson, and several others, the feeling was different. Their sad and downcast looks betrayed an uneasy conscience. They were experiencing something of the effects of "coals of fire on their heads." Their remorse was increased by the belief that their teacher knew of their treatment to Mellie, and intended a personal application of his remarks. The young ladies were not heartless and unkind, but they were gay and thoughtless. Like many of my young readers, they were impulsive and hasty.

Thoughtlessness, however, is a great evil, and

often leads to follies whose fruit is a long and bitter repentance. The indulgence of envious and malicious dispositions is seldom followed by pleasant results. But the girls were fairly conquered by kindness; they formed the just and sensible resolution that they would rise by their own exertions, and stand on their own merits, and that they would never again be guilty of an act so dishonorable as trying to injure the good name of a meritorious little school-mate—they would never again attempt to rise by the downfall of another.

At recess several of the girls went to Mellie with confessions of sorrow, and told her that "her kind treatment, together with Mr. Hamilton's lecture, had made them feel so badly that they could not study their lessons, without first confessing their faults and asking her forgiveness.

Mellie threw back her flowing hair, that now hung in tresses over her face, and with large tear-drops chasing each other from her full blue eyes, threw her arms around each in turn, and pressed upon them a warm kiss of true affection and forgiveness. Not a word did she utter. Her heart was so full she could not speak. But so magical was the effect upon the others, that they were forced to give vent to their feelings in sobs and tears.

Mr. Hamilton came in just in time to learn the situation, and said that it seemed that his remarks in the morning must have been providentially directed, as he himself was at the time ignorant of what had previously passed among his pupils. From this time forward the most perfect harmony prevailed in the school. Jealousy, that hideous monster, that had crept in, was now effectually killed, and Peace was restored to its rightful possession. Each now seemed to vie with the other as to who could do her own part best. They were all kind to each other. They no longer sought to detract anything from little Mellie, hence she was again the general favorite of the school. With pride Mr. Hamilton often boasted of his well disciplined, orderly and harmonious school; and had but little trouble, either from the indolence or other misconduct, of his pupils.

Mellie continued at school three years, making rapid progress all the time. For brilliancy and vigor of mind, she had no equal. The gratuitous titles conferred on her, of "Little Inquisitive" and "Little Baptist," if not deserved, were accepted by her with marked approval. Especially the latter, by which she became widely known, was appreciated as a most agreeable distinction. When teased by her companions for being a "Little Baptist," she would reply: "If I do become a Baptist, it will be because the Bible makes me a Baptist. If the Bible does make me a Baptist, why, then, I'll be a Baptist—*that's all.*" Thus she would reason, feeling fully conscious that no blame could be attached to her for following the teachings of the Bible, notwithstanding she might go contrary to the wishes of her dearest friends.

Without presuming to present her conclusions

as infallible, yet she is a most worthy example, in that she takes the Bible for her teacher, and resolves to be led by its instructions, regardless of the opinions of her church or people. She exhibits a child-like simplicity and confidence that should actuate all of God's intelligent creatures. Like the little Samuel of old, she was ready to say, "Speak Lord, for thy servant heareth." She fully recognized that it is God's province to command, and each individual's duty to obey.

CHAPTER VI.

MELLIE AT HOME—THE BAPTIST MEETING.

AFTER being three years in school, Mellie's parents thought best to keep her at home awhile, that her mind might rest from incessant study. They wisely judged that relaxation was necessary to expand and strengthen her mind. The mind is like the *bow*, if never unstrung, it will lose its elasticity; and it is well that parents pay some attention to the physical, as well as the mental and moral development of their children.

Fortunately, Mrs. Brown did not entertain any of those "straight-laced" notions that would keep a child in seclusion and force it to grow up as a "hot-house plant," deprived of the benefits of sun and air, but, encouraged her children in outdoor exercises. She trained them to habits of industry, and allowed them to run and romp upon the green grass, to ramble in the woods, along the brooks and over the hills, thus cultivating their physical nature. If her children wished to strengthen their voices by singing or hallooing, she did not deem it any violation of propriety. For she would say, "to let children be children is the only way to make them grow up healthy and useful men and women."

After so long confinement in the village school house, Mellie derived great pleasure from outdoor exercises. She, too, took a deep interest in everything relative to the household. The affairs of the kitchen, the garden and the flowers, gave her much pleasant employment. She daily looked after the ducks and chickens, hunted the nests and nourished the young, thus making her time profitable as well as pleasant. She was ever kind to her little sister, who was now large enough to accompany her out to gather flowers, watch the birds, and engage in other amusements. When she became tired of play, she would resort to her books, by which means she advanced some in her studies, beside reading many histories and other valuable books, from which she stored her mind with valuable knowledge. Her Bible, too, was not neglected; but from this she learned new truth day by day. Not confining her investigations by any means to the subject of baptism, she gave to this some attention. The more she read, and the older she grew, the stronger were her convictions that the Bible was, indeed, "a Baptist book." She read and re-read, and pencil marked every text having any allusion to the subject. At her request, her mother agreed to help her to examine in detail every place where baptism was mentioned, and she had all arranged so as to turn to any given text at pleasure.

Frank Brown had been three years at college, but was now at home for a few weeks, when he would return one more year before graduating. He had grown to be a man, and was much improved in appearance. Mrs. Brown felt that no mother was ever blessed with a nobler son, or a more sprightly daughter. Except little Anna, who was then prattling around her knees, these were her only surviving children. Death had taken off several in their infancy, and it is not strange, therefore, that her affections were set, almost to idolatry, on the surviving ones.

Col. Brown being a man of business, and much of his time away from home, the chief responsibility of training the children devolved upon his wife. She was, however, aided much by his counsels; and her course with them was mainly in accordance with their mutual convictions and plans. Yet, from a greater intimacy with their mother, and her sympathies entering at all times more fully into theirs, the children looked almost exclusively to her for counsel. Therefore, the first impressions were made by the mother. She instilled into their minds principles of the strictest virtue and morality, and had labored to arm them with courage against everything of a dishonorable character. She admonished them to always have the courage to do right, and to resist every temptation to any act low or dishonorable. Thus she molded the characters of her offspring while their minds where tender and easily impressed.

Frank had not been long at home, until Mellie told him how distressed she was on reading the Bible that he gave her the day before he started to college; and how she thought he had made a mistake and given her a Baptist Bible; and how mother had convinced her that it was just like any other Bible, and how the school-girls had called her a little Baptist, because she told them that the Bible was a Baptist book; and many other things that had transpired during his absence. Then she told him that "mamma" was going to help her, and they were intending to examine every place in the New Testament where any account was given of persons' being baptized, and she would find out for herself whether the New Testament people were Baptists or Presbyterians.

"But, Mell, suppose you should find that the New Testament people, as you call them, were Baptists," said Frank, "what then?"

"Why, then," replied Mellie, "I'll be a Baptist myself—that's what."

"Pshaw," said Frank, "you surprise me!"

"Now, don't you remember, Buddie," said Mellie, "that when you gave me my Bible, you told me to read it, and that it would tell me what I must do to be good; and that I must obey all that it said and be a good girl? And now, Buddie, don't you want me to do whatever it tells me?"

"O, yes, Mell," said Frank, "but I rather think you are too young yet to set yourself up as a judge of Bible doctrines; notwithstanding, I must confess that you reason like a little philosopher. But as it is the Sabbath day we will not enter into any further discussion. When you and mother begin your investigation of baptism, I will join you, and maybe between us, we can arrive at a correct conclusion. I hope that we will at least get these Baptist notions out of your head."

"All right, Buddie, we'll begin on Monday morning," said Mellie, in a gleeful mood, seeming wholly indifferent as to what the result should be, only so she arrived at the truth. The ringing of the bell at the Baptist church caused Frank to start from his seat. He remarked to his mother that he would go to church; that as Dr. Farnsworth was sick, and the Methodist minister was away, all the people would go to the Baptist church, and that as he wished to see all his friends after his long absence," going to the Baptist church was *the very idea.*

"Mellie came running to ask "mamma" to let her "go with Buddie to the Baptist meeting;" and Mrs. Brown said that she would go along too; "For," said she, "Mr. Coleman preaches some very good sermons, and I like to hear him, *if he is a Baptist.*"

Arriving at the church they found a large congregation. The house could not seat all the people and some stood up while others were forced to go away.

Although the Baptists had had an unfavorable beginning in the town, they had steadily increased until they now numbered more actual members than any other denomination in the place, and had received into their communion some of the best and most influential citizens of the community. When Mr. Coleman first settled among them, he was quite a young man, and for a time attracted but little attention from people outside his own church; but being a man of great energy and unblemished piety, he made great improvement, and had remarkable success. He was now, as a pulpit orator, second to no minister in the place, although the Presbyterian pastor had been favored with a thorough literary and theological course, and had also been honored with the title of Doctor of Divinity.

On this occasion, Mr. Coleman preached a very plain, practical sermon, earnest and Scriptural. His theme was "The Spirituality of the Christian Religion;" in comparison with which Priest-craft and Ritualism suffered severely. He removed all the supports from those who were trusting in ordinances and outward performances, and showed most clearly that true religion had to do with the heart—the affections, and not with outward show. That to be saved required an internal condition, produced not by external service, but by the renewing of the Holy Spirit.

The sermon ended, he announced that after a few moments for preparation he would attend to the ordinance of baptism. And while he had gone into the vestry to prepare for the service, two of his deacons rolled back the pulpit, exposing to view a beautiful font of pure water. The pastor made but few remarks, only saying that "in the earliest age of Christianity, streams and lakes were usually resorted to, but the essential object was to have a sufficiency of water in which to perform the action of baptism. But we may go back far into the past, even to the latter days of the apostles, and there we find that baptisteries were especially prepared simply because it is more convenient to perform this service in the church, and the purpose is as well answered as if in the Jordan, in whose waters the Saviour was baptized. The object of baptism is obedience to Christ; the action is to declare, *emblematically*, a death to sin and a resurrection to a new life. Three things are necessary to Scriptural Baptism: First, a qualified officer of the church to administer it; secondly, a believing subject; thirdly, *an immersion in water.*"

When the candidate came forward, it was none other than Laura Thompson, little Mellie's school-mate, who had been the first to call her the "Little Baptist." The minister took her. As they came up out of the water, while a profound silence reigned throughout the congregation, little Mellie said, "Mamma, that looks like the Bible way of doing it;" to which Mrs. Brown only replied by biting her lips and shaking her head, giving Mellie to understand that it was not a proper time nor place for remarks. Although Mellie was noted for precision of manners, there were times when it seemed impossible for her to prevent her tongue from speaking the thoughts of her mind.

CHAPTER VII.

THE INVESTIGATION.

MONDAY morning found Mellie engaged helping to get the housework done, so that everything might be in readiness for the examination of the subject of baptism. When through with the work, she arranged her toilet, fixed some flowers in her hair, then got her Bible, and said: "Come now, Buddie, you and mamma, and I'll show you what makes me a little Baptist. But, then, if you will convince me that I don't understand the book, I will not be a little Baptist any longer. I was so glad to see Laura Thompson baptized, and I did want to go to her and kiss her when she came out of the water—she did look so sweet and so happy, but there were so many people around her, I could not get to her. She didn't look happy that way when Mr. Hamilton lectured us about doing good for evil."

"No doubt," replied Mrs. Brown, "Laura is a very good girl, but I don't see any use for going to all the trouble of having a great pool of water to put her all over in, when a few drops would have done just as well."

"But, mamma," returned Mellie, "that's just like the Bible way of baptizing people—just for all the world, it is, and people ought to follow the teachings of the Bible, if it is some trouble. Now look here."

Mellie opened her Bible at the third chapter of Matthew, where occurs the first mention of baptism, and said: "Now see how it reads: the people went to John, the Baptist, and were baptized of him *'in* Jordan;' and then in the sixteenth verse it reads: 'And Jesus, when he was baptized, came up straightway *out of the water,'* just for all the world like Laura Thompson did yesterday. Then the Saviour says: 'If any man will be my disciple, let him deny himself, and take up his cross and follow me;' and, mamma, I think that that was what made Laura Thompson look so happy yesterday; she was following the Saviour in obedience to His command, and she felt pleasant in the path of duty, for 'wisdom's ways are ways of pleasantness, and all her paths are peace.'"

"Well, Mell, go on, dear," said Mrs. Brown, "and let us see how many witnesses you can find on the Baptist side. I intend that you shall decide the question for yourself. Your father says that he has a great curiosity to know what will be your conclusion after an impartial investigation. He said that had he not been compelled to go away on business, he would have stayed with us, and assisted us to arrive at an unprejudiced decision."

"But, Mellie," said Frank, "to save the trouble of turning back and going over the same ground twice, let us examine the evidence on both sides of the question. Look at the eleventh verse, it says, 'I baptize you *with* water.' Now, if John, the Baptist, baptized the people *with* water, is it not plain that he put the water on them, instead of putting them into the water?"

"No, Buddie, if it did not say, 'they went down into the water,' and that they were baptized in the river, then, maybe, we would not know how it was done; but the Bible is too plain, Buddie. John said he baptized with water: distinguishing the water from the Holy Ghost, with which he said Christ would baptize them. And, yet, when anyone baptizes in water, don't they baptize *with* water? When you saw Laura Thompson covered up in the water, could you not as well say, 'She was covered with water? Either is proper. Mamma, didn't Polly, this morning, scald the chicken with hot water, and didn't she put the chicken in the water?"

"O, but hold on, Mell, the Bible don't say that John baptized the people in the river, it only says it was in Jordan; and how do you know but that Jordan was the name of a town or a place in some dry country?" replied Frank, more disposed to tease his sister than to give her instruction.

"Yes, but it does say that it was a river, somewhere,' rejoined Mellie; and, quick as thought, she turned to the first chapter of Mark, and read:" And there went out unto him all the land of Judea, and they of Jerusalem, and were all baptized of him in the river Jordan, confessing their sins." And again she read: "And it came to pass in those days, that Jesus came from Nazareth of Galilee, and was baptized of John *in*

Jordan." Now, Buddie, don't this prove that Jordan is a river, and that the people were all baptized *in* the river? And haven't I read in my geography about the river Jordan, and haven't I seen it on my map of the Holy Land? Let us take mamma's advice, and 'have the courage to stick to the truth,' Buddie."

Without waiting to hear any reply, Mellie ran into her father's library, and returned with a large book, called "Lynch's Expedition to the Holy Land." For, young as she was, she was familiar with almost every book in the library. "Look here," said she, "the man that wrote this book has been to Jordan, and traveled down it in a boat, and he ought to know whether it's a river or not; and I guess he was no Baptist: he was an officer of the United States Navy, and was sent out by the government. The people there showed him the very place where they said Christ was baptized. Now just see what he wrote while standing on the bank of the river looking at the water, and thinking about the Saviour having been baptized there: 'The mind of man trammeled by sin, cannot soar in contemplation of so sublime an event. On that wondrous day, when the Deity, veiled in flesh, descended the bank, all nature, hushed in awe, looked on—and the impetuous river, in grateful homage, must have stayed its course, and gently laved the body of its Lord.'" Mellie read this with a solemn air, giving particular emphasis to the words, "impetuous river," and gently laving the body of its Lord."

Frank listened in silence, and Mrs. Brown

seemed wholly unconscious that her knitting had fallen from her hands, so great was her amazement at the ease with which Mellie seemed to manage the subject.

While Mellie had looked a mere child, she showed a remarkably quick perception, and was capable of solid reasoning. Though only in her fourteenth year, her mind was well cultivated, surpassing even many full grown men and women. So small, with such extra-ordinary knowledge, she was regarded, as indeed, a prodigy. The intention of her mother was to gratify Mellie and to amuse herself, contemplating no other result than a little pastime; but at every step her astonishment increased at the plain light in which she exhibited the subject of baptism, over which so many Doctors have disagreed.

Seeing that her mother and Frank did not question her testimony, Mellie turned to the eighth chapter of Acts and read: "And they went down both into the water, both Philip and the Eunuch; and he baptized him. And when they were come up out of the water, the Spirit of the Lord caught away Philip," etc. She continued: "Now, Buddie, you see that Philip went with the man into the water, and there, in the water, he baptized him, and then, both came up out of the water; and that's what made me ask Mr. Hamilton if Philip was not a Baptist. He did just like Mr. Coleman does when he baptizes people. Then the girls made fun of me, and called me 'The Little Baptist.' Now I know I am only a little girl, and not old enough to know everything, yet when I see anything *so plain*, I think I can understand it. Mamma says that holy men wrote the Bible, just as God directed them, and that God gave us the Bible to teach us our duty, so I think He must have meant for us to understand what He wants us to do, and then to do just what He commands. I'm so glad that you gave me my Bible, Buddie; I've learned so much from it; and I want to do all that it tells me."

"Well, Mell," said Frank, "I see that you are determined to be a Baptist in spite of all we can do; but don't you know that when anybody gets into the Baptist church there is no way for them to get out again?"

"Why can't I get out Buddie, if I want to," said Mellie.

"Because," said Frank, "they take their members in through the water, and I don't see how they can ever get out. I never heard of any other door to the church; so I suppose they have to remain there until they die out, unless they can be taken backward through the water again."

"Sprinkle 'em out, Buddie, sprinkle 'em out. Why, Buddie, don't you know dey sprinkle 'em?"

This was the prattle of little Anna, who had been playing on the floor unobserved, until she called out, "Sprinkle 'em out, Buddie, sprinkle 'em out."

She understood that the Baptist would not have "sprinkled" members; and as that formed a line of separation, she drew the conclusion that sprinkling their members would put them out of the church.

This interrupted the discussion for the time, and created laughter. Frank said that he would *hush*. Mellie laughed till the tears stood in her eyes. Mrs. Brown caressed Anna, and awarded her a high honor for the original and very novel idea of sprinkling the Baptists to get them out of the church.

Mellie had not thought as much on the subject of the door into the church, as she had about some other things, else she might have told Frank that baptism is not, strictly speaking, a door, but the initiatory rite that all entering the church are required to submit to, but the door that opens or closes against them is the WILL of the particular church. Thus, ingress and egress are obtained by the same door. Churches vote to receive members and they vote to exclude members. Each church is independent of all human authority, and subject only to her great Head and Lawgiver.

Frank Brown had never given the subject of baptism an hour's serious consideration, and at this time cared for little else than to annoy his sister with such difficulties as he could remember hearing suggested by others. He had been told that he had been baptized in his infancy, an act of his parents which he understood to somehow bring him into some kind of a covenant relation with God. Although unexplained he doubted not that there was some virtue to be derived from a practice to which so much importance was attached by the church in which he had grown up as a "sealed" member. He was moral, paid respect to the Sabbath, attended church, but was yet irreligious. After the discussion with Mellie had been suspended, he sat as if wholly absorbed in thought, turning the leaves of the little Bible until he was attracted by some marks that Mellie had made in the sixteenth chapter of Acts, and he said:

"Look here, Sissie: you have made your strong points; all that you can find, I guess; so now let us examine the other side of the question. Here I see there was a baptism in a prison, and in the night, too. I hope you do not presume that they had a river there. I think that this is one case where you will have to admit that there was no immersion. If you have proved that Philip was a Baptist, I will now prove that Paul was a Presbyterian. For, you see, they had Paul confined in the inner prison, and when the jailer asked, 'What must I do to be saved?' and Paul told him to believe on the Lord Jesus Christ, etc., that then and there Paul baptized him."

Mellie replied, "Yes, Buddie, don't you see how it reads? The jailer brought Paul and Silas out of the prison, and they spake the word of the Lord to him and all that were in his house. They were not in the jailer's house for they had come out of the prison. Then the jailer took them and washed their stripes; and was baptized. Now, don't it look reasonable that he took them where there was water to wash their stripes'—to some stream or pool? After washing their stripes he was baptized. And after he had brought them into his house again, he set meat before them; so you see the jailer was not baptized in the house. But suppose they never went outside the prison walls, could there not have been a pool there to furnish water for the prison? When the Bible tells how anyone was baptized, it is always in a river or a place of much water; and where it just says 'they were baptized,' we ought to be satisfied that it was all done the same way. Now turn to the third chapter of John; there it says that 'John (the Baptist) was baptizing in Enon, near to Salim, because there was much water there.' Now, if it required much water for John to baptize the people, don't you think it would have required *much* water for Paul to baptize the jailer? If you had not gone to church on yesterday, and had been told that Laura Thompson was baptized in the meeting house, you would never have thought, perhaps, that she was immersed. For you would have thought, no doubt, that there was not water enough there for that. but when the pulpit was rolled back, you saw a pool of water—a baptistery they call it—and it is no more strange that there should be such a thing within the walls of a prison, than in a meeting-house."

"O, but I tell you, Mellie," said Frank, "Paul *was* a Presbyterian, because *he* was not baptized in any of your rivers, nor pools either. I have read about it somewhere myself, and I remember to have heard Dr. Farnsworth say that 'the presumption is very strong that Paul was baptized either by sprinkling or pouring, and that too, while he was standing on his feet.' And you remember that when Dr. Farnsworth baptized Mr. Snyder, he said: 'As Ananias said unto Paul, Arise and be baptized;' and when Mr. Snyder stood on his feet while Dr. Farnsworth poured the water on his head, it fixed the impression on my mind that that was the way Paul was baptized. But, here, take the book and find the place—we'll read it."

"Yes, I have it marked," said Mellie, "it's in the ninth chapter of Acts. After Ananias had gone to him, 'he received sight forthwith, and arose, and was baptized.' Then, again, in the twenty-second chapter, Paul says himself that Ananias said unto him: 'Why tarriest thou? arise, and be baptized,' etc."

"Well," said Frank, "do you see any immersion in this? Won't Paul do for a Presbyterian? He was baptized just like Dr. Farnsworth baptized Mr. Snyder."

"No proof, no proof in the book, Buddie," said Mellie. "If he were only sprinkled, it would not have been necessary for him to arise, yet he *must* have arisen in order to have been immersed; and Ananias' question, 'Why tarriest thou?' shows that it was necessary for him to get up and go with Ananias to some place, But, then, let us take another view of the subject. We have already seen that Christ was baptized in the river Jordan, and Paul being a follower of Christ, was, of course, baptized in the same way that Christ himself was. This ought to be conceded, unless there is positive proof to the contrary, which we fail to find. But, then, I guess that Paul is capable of settling this dispute. He surely knew himself how he was baptized, and how others in his day were baptized. So we will take his answer from the sixth chapter of Romans. Hear, now, what he says: 'So many of us as were baptized into Jesus Christ, were baptized into his death; therefore we are buried with him by baptism,' etc. Again, he reminds the Colossians, in second chapter and twelfth verse, that they were 'Buried with him (Christ) in baptism,' and says to them, 'Wherein also ye are risen with him through the faith of the operation of God, who hath raised him from the dead.' And I tell you now that Paul will not begin to do for a Presbyterian, but he was a Baptist, all over. He proved that himself; the jailer, and the Christians to whom he was writing, were all buried by baptism. So I say that Philip was a Baptist, and that Paul was just as good a Baptist as Philip, and that they both baptized just like John, the Baptist, did, and like the Baptist people do now—just like you saw Mr. Coleman baptize yesterday."

"Nonsense, Mellie, nonsense," replied Frank sarcastically. "Buried in baptism is only a figurative expression. No allusion is had to water baptism, at all. I have heard this explained often. Paul was talking about the baptism of the Spirit, and not about literal baptism. You must remember that much of the Bible is given to us in figurative language, and must not be interpreted literally."

"La! la! Buddie," said Mellie, "have you been

all this time in college, and never learned that figures are always representative? Why, Mr. Hamilton taught me this before I had been in his school six months, that a figure is like a picture, and as such must represent something. You can't have a shadow without a substance nor can you express a figurative idea, without first having in view the thing from which the figure is drawn. Mr. Hamilton made this all so plain that I have never forgotten it; and mamma has taught me a great deal about the figures of speech in the Bible. Why, before I understood this, I could not make any sense out of many texts that I read. I found that in one place Christ was called the Sun, in another a Rock, and still in another the Door, but when mamma explained it to me it was all plain. I understood the nature of the sun, of the rock, and of a door, and could see at once how the figures conveyed the ideas. Then mamma explained to me what David in the Psalms meant when he talked about being overwhelmed with troubles, and when I got started in it I could understand a great many of the figures of speech. I could then understand that the reason Christ called His sufferings a baptism, was because they were overwhelming. So, now, if Paul used a figure of speech to explain the work of the Holy Spirit, when he said, 'We are buried with Christ by baptism,' it then follows that the literal baptism is a burial also. If baptism is a literal burial and raising up, then I can understand the figure drawn from it to be a baptism too, when the idea expressed is going from death unto life.

If Paul were speaking about baptism in water, of course he meant immersion, and if the work of the Holy Spirit was meant, and figuratively called a burial, it is just as strong—*just as positive proof*. If the figure of water baptism is a burial, that proves that the baptism is like that. So you may take it any way you please, but if you will only take it according to the laws of language on every other subject, you will find that the Bible means immersion every time baptism is mentioned."

"Well, Mell," said Frank, "if you are distinguished for any one thing in particular, it is for having a good memory. You have not only repeated Mr. Hamilton's lecture on figurative language, but you have supplemented it with some Baptist preacher's sermon. I think we had better adjourn now for a little recreation."

"All right," said Mellie, "if you are tired we'll stop, but I have been too much interested to think about getting tired. I want to find out the *truth*; you know, Buddie, we should 'buy the truth and sell it not.' But what do you say about figurative language being always drawn from literal speech, like the shadow from the substance?"

"Well, I guess that is according to the books — I will study more about it," replied Frank, and the conversation ended.

CHAPTER VIII.

THE COUNTRY—DR. FARNSWORTH'S VISIT—
BIBLE PICTURES.

DURING Frank's stay at home, much of the time of the family was spent in entertaining company and returning visits. Mellie's time being thus employed, she ceased to annoy them with questions about her "Baptist Bible," as she always called it. Her mother permitted her to go with Frank to visit her aunts and cousins in the country; a trip which pleased her very much, and of which she had much to tell when she returned. She was greatly attracted by country life. She loved the trees and the flowers—loved to gather the fruits with her own hands. She delighted to ramble amid the groves, to watch the fishes in the gleeful brook, and to see the birds fitting about their nests and heeding the cries of their young.

The country seemed to Mellie a real paradise, compared with the hot and dusty town. She would entreat her mother to "persuade papa to move to the country where everything is so delightful." She wanted to feast her eyes upon the growing crops of cotton and corn, and the waving harvest, and to see the toiling husbandmen tilling the ground and mowing the hay; and, then, there were the fruits, the melons, and many other attractions.

One day she said, "Mamma, you have always taught me that God made the whole world and everything that we see, but I can but wonder why He made so many things. It looks like there are more things in the world than are of any use."

"God has a purpose, my dear, in all that He has made, and He intends all for the good of His creatures. He is very kind to arrange everything to suit our wants, and we ought to be very thankful for it, and to love Him, and be obedient to Him, because of all these blessings."

"But God don't make the corn and the cotton; men work in the fields and make these things, don't they, mamma?"

"God has commanded us all to work. He does not want us to be idle, but to be always usefully employed. He has so arranged the laws of nature that if men do not cultivate the ground, the fields and gardens will not produce the needful crops; yet remember that we can't make a single stalk of corn grow. Men can sow the seeds and cultivate the ground, but unless God sends the sunshine and the rain, and causes the seasons to come in their order, there will be no crops. So if God did not help us, we would soon perish in spite of all the work we would do. God commands us to work, and when we obey Him, He blesses our labors, and rewards us with the harvest. Then, when we have labored and procured enough of the good things of this world to satisfy our wants, we ought to thank God for it all, because it is only through His kindness and mercy that we have obtained it. Don't you understand this, Mellie?"

"Yes, mamma, I see how it is. God tells us just what He wants us to do, and if we obey Him, He rewards us with His blessings, but if we are lazy, and do not obey Him, He is displeased with us, and will let us suffer. I can't make a blade of grass grow, nor a grain of corn sprout—nor a pretty flower open, but I can do what God tells me to do and then trust Him for the balance. *That's the idea*; I see how it is. I remember that I have read in my Bible that God is angry with the wicked every day, and He don't like lazy people much better, for He says they shall beg in the harvest, and have nothing. I intend to be good, and to be industrious. I won't be wicked nor lazy."

Saying this, she bounded from the room and ran out into the yard to where there was a fuss among the ducks and chickens, and Mrs. Brown went about packing Frank's trunk, preparatory to his return to college. She regretted the returning necessity for Frank's absence, but she hoped that he would make a wise and useful man, and, therefore, she wanted him to have all the advantages that a good education would give him. She was willing to sacrifice the pleasure of his presence at home, while he should finish his course at college.

Early in the morning everything was in readiness, and with tearful eyes, Frank took his leave of the family, and hurried off to meet the train which was to carry him far away.

Dr. Farnsworth called at Col. Brown's that morning for the purpose of "consoling sister Brown upon the departure of her son," but with a secret purpose of checking, what he termed, "Mellie's heretical notions about baptism." After the usual congratulations and a few minutes spent in conversation of a general character, he remarked:

"I am very sorry to hear reports sister Brown, that are afloat in the community, to the effect that your little daughter is becoming an open defender of the Baptists. It is said that she boldly and publicly declares that the Bible is a Baptist book. She has a great influence over the children of the church, and, I am told, has actually made some of them believe that they have not been baptized, or, at least, that their baptism is not Scriptural. If she persists in this course, she will do our church an injury —and this I am far from believing will have your encouragement. I assure you that I do not express these fears without cause, and, as your pastor, your friend, and the friend of your child, I would willingly assist you in correcting her opinions before she gets beyond the reach of our influence. For if we do not get these notions out of her head now, they will become settled there, and she will grow up a confirmed Baptist, which, I am sure, would be no less mortifying to you than to myself."

"Dr. Farnsworth," said Mrs. Brown, "I am far from intentionally doing anything to injure my child, or to bring trouble upon the church, but

Mellie has taken up these notions without any influence in that direction being exerted upon her, only as she formed conclusions from reading the Bible. I was much surprised at it at first, but regarded it as only a childish whim, and expecting that nothing *serious* would grow out of it, I have indulged her in it, not really so much for her gratification, as to see what impression the Bible would make on a mind free from all prejudice. I must confess that the result has surprised me truly, for the more she reads, the stronger she becomes in her first impressions. So I do not know what is to come of it *finally*."

This last sentence was spoken in a manner that showed but little concern if it should turn out even according to the pastor's fears.

Dr. Farnsworth remarked:

"But, sister Brown, (*ahem!*) I would not mention this to any one but yourself, but as your pastor, I must in kindness tell you that rumor says that you have not only indulged Mellie in these wild fancies, but that you have encouraged her in them. I hope, however, that this is a mistake. I have repeatedly taken upon myself the responsibility of contradicting the report, and said that such a thing could not be; that you were one of our best members, and surely could not so far forget your duty to the church as to sanction the course your child is pursuing."

"It is true," she said, "I have encouraged Mellie to read her Bible, but have said nothing to influence her conclusions in reference to baptism. I have been studiously guarded in this and have left her mind entirely free."

"There is where you have committed a grave error, sister Brown. Now, of course, we must not prevent our children from reading the Bible, yet we should keep a strict watch over them and try to keep their minds under such discipline as will insure them against the danger of imbibing false notions. And it would be well if Mellie could be influenced to let the Bible alone awhile. Let her read some of our denominational literature until her mind becomes more settled. Of course I would not say this publicly, nor would I, as a general thing, discourage a free reading of the Bible; but the reading of other works are needed as helps to understand it. See that she reads the Catechism, and other books in which our doctrines are set forth. Solomon said, 'Train up a child in the way he should go, and when he is old he will not depart from it.' If we just give our children the Bible without instructing them in its meaning, threefourths of them will come out Baptists in the end. So, if we want them to be Presbyterians, we must indoctrinate them in our faith while their minds are easily impressed; for, you know, that

> 'Education forms the common mind;
> As the twig is bent, so is the tree inclined.'

Impressions made on the minds of children are seldom erased."

"Who would have thought it possible," said Mrs. Brown, "for a child of Mellie's age to have turned the world upside down by a little reading of the Bible? It is something wonderful if her childish prattle about baptism, and the Baptist Bible, is going to turn the heads of all the children in the town and make *crazy little Baptists of them.* But, Dr. Farnsworth, you insinuate that I have neglected my duty in not having Mellie more familiar with our church Catechism. Now, sir, *that's just what's the matter*—she knows too much about the Catechism. When she found the Bible differing from the teachings of her Catechism, she decided at once that her's was a Baptist Bible, and there is where all this trouble started. When convinced that her Bible was the same as others, and that God was the author of the Bible, and man the author of the Catechism, she readily accepted the Bible and adhered to its teachings."

Mrs. Brown spoke in rather an animated spirit, and the doctor thought her tone was a little sharp. It was the first time she had ever heard her pastor insinuate that the doctrines of her church were in danger from a too free use of the Bible; and the suggestion that she should restrain her child from reading it, she regarded as indeed strange—coming from one who professed to take the Bible for his *rule* in both faith and practice.

Dr. Farnsworth was somewhat confused at the effect his remarks were seeming to have, but recovering his balance, he continued, "Sister Brown, I would by no means have you to understand me as wishing to dictate to you in this matter, but I see clearly that you do not conceive the extent of Mellie's influence, nor the danger there is of her leaving the church in which she was born and dedicated to God by baptism, as well as of leading astray so many other children. For, young as she is her opinions have great weight with the people. You know that I design no flattery to you, by saying that she is an extraordinary child, and manifests unusual knowledge for a person of her age, so much so, that many regard her as being almost supernatural. And *just the idea* that a child left unbiased to read the Scriptures, sees everything in favor of the Baptists, carries great force with it. It naturally creates the impression that the Bible is so plainly in favor of Baptists' peculiar views that every one would become a Baptist if they would read without prejudice."

Mrs. Brown was about to reply that if she thought such was the case, she would envy the Baptists' position, but Mellie entered the room at the time, and she thought it more prudent to suspend her remarks until another time.

Dr. Farnsworth looked at his watch and discovered that he had overstayed his time; asked to be excused, and promised to call another day. Turning to leave, he took a nicely bound little book from his pocket, saying: "Here, Mellie, you are fond of reading new books, and I have one that I will leave for you, and when I call again you must tell me how many nice things you have found in it."

"Thank you, Doctor," said Mellie, receiving the book with a smile that told how proud she felt for such a token of the Doctor's regard.

Dr. Farnsworth bid all a good-bye, patted Mellie on the head, telling her to be a good girl; to read her new book carefully, and then, mounting his horse, rode away.

As soon as Dr. Farnsworth had gone, Mellie said: "Mamma, I'll read this new book, but before I begin, I want you to tell me about the pictures in the Bible. Some Bibles have pictures and others have not; and if God made the pictures or had them put in the Bible, why are they not in all alike?"

"Pictures," said her mother, "are the inventions of man. God did not make them nor instruct man to put them in the Bible; therefore pictures representing men and things are in some Bibles and in others they are not."

"Well, then," said Mellie, "Mrs. McFlimsey, the Methodist Sunday School teacher, tried to deceive me, and I don't think it was honest in her to do it. You see I told her that Christ was baptized in the river by immersion, and she said He was not, but that the water was poured on Him. I asked her to prove it by the Bible, and she went and got a Bible that had a picture of one man pouring water out of a horn on another man, and says she, 'Here is John the Baptist pouring water on Christ out of a horn, and you can't dispute it, for it is plain before your eyes, *in the Bible.*' The Sunday School children all believed it, but it was so different from the reading that I could not see how it could be true and have been greatly puzzled about it, and wanted you to tell me about it. I guess the reading don't suit some folks, and they make pictures in the Bible to try to make children believe things that are not taught there. Well, I'm glad there are no pictures in my Bible, so I have nothing to hinder me from believing the truth just as God has told it."

CHAPTER IX.

REFLECTIONS-CONVERSATION-VISITORS,

THE pastor's remarks weighed heavily with Mrs. Brown. Reflections and misgivings were aroused that had never before entered her mind. She could only interpret certain expressions to mean that a too free use of the Bible was dangerous to certain tenets of her church. She had been a church member twenty years, and such a thought had never before entered her mind. She had not even allowed herself to doubt that the Bible was the reliance of her church for the defense of its practice. These reflections gave her great trouble. Had she been all her life mistaken? Instead of following God's truth, had she been only following the creeds of men? Was Mellie's conclusion indeed correct, that the Bible is a Baptist book? Such questions as these passed hastily through her mind. She here resolved to study the Bible more thoroughly than she had heretofore done, and by God's assistance to follow its teachings.

Like thousands of others, she had trusted the opinions of fallible men, instead of going directly to the fountain of all truth to learn her duty. Mellie's argument had paved the way for this decision, yet it might never have been fully reached had not her pastor's visit resulted in a further shaking of her faith in the creed of her church.

The little book that Dr. Farnsworth gave Mellie, proved, on examination, to be a defense of the practice of the Pedobaptists, and was considered as a masterly argument, both for the infant rite and for sprinkling and pouring as the action of baptism. Mellie devoted all her spare time to the book until she had reached the end. But, while reading it, she kept her little Bible by her side, and would turn and read all the references given, so that when she had gone through comparing the teachings of one with the other, she had also learned much in the Bible, and the result was that her confidence in it as a Baptist book was not in the least shaken. Her mother said but little to her concerning the new book, because she thought that as Mellie was so quick to observe every expression in the Bible, favoring the Baptist ground, if this work was conclusive against it, her quick perception would enable her to discern it. But one day Mellie said: "Mamma, what do you think Dr. Farnsworth gave me this book for? I've read it all, over and over, and it talks all the time about baptisms, covenants, dedications and sealing ordinances, and I *can't see the point.*"

"Why, my dear," answered Mrs. Brown, "I thought that you had been studying the subject until you could understand all about baptism."

"Yes, yes, mamma, I can understand it in my Bible--it's so plain there. It's not mixed up with all these things about circumcision, covenants and sealing ordinances—and a dozen things that nobody can see any reason in. I believe that the man who made this book did it just to confuse people's minds, so as to keep them from understanding the Bible. Mamma, I don't want to believe anything that needs so much explanation and *mystification*. So I will just believe my Bible for I can understand a good deal of it now, and I'll keep on trying to learn more about it. The Bible is God's book, and all He has put into it is right; and if Dr. Farnsworth meant what he said when he preached about the duty of people to do as God commands them, why don't he want them to learn from God's book, and not be giving them books that some man has made so mysterious that they can't understand them? I don't like a book that tries to explain away the plain words of my Bible. I guess that God knows just what He wants us to do, and tells us so plainly that we can understand it." Mrs. Brown suggested to Mellie that, perhaps, she was too young to understand all these things correctly, and advised her to let the subject rest until she was older, and to employ her time on her school books, telling her that it would not be long until she must go off to school.

When school was mentioned, Mellie replied:

"That will just suit me, mamma; papa said I must stay at home one year, and then I should go to school two years. I guess it is nearly time for me to go. I wish papa would let me go to the country to school. I love to stay in the country where I can see the trees and birds, and the pretty wild flowers; and where I can gather berries and fruits, like I did when Buddie and I went to Aunt Julia's last summer. O it would be so nice! Won't you persuade papa to let me go to the country to school?"

The entrance of Laura Thompson and her mother put a stop to the conversation, and while Mrs. Brown and Mrs. Thompson engaged in a regular chat, Mellie and Laura took a walk, first into the garden, then to see the young chickens, and finally back into the library. In looking around the room, Laura soon discovered Mellie's new book on baptism, and began to turn the leaves and to examine its contents. Mellie told her all about Dr. Farnsworth giving it to her, and the opinion she had formed of it, and her determination to stick to her Bible.

"Well, I declare, Mell," said Laura, "here's that little 'Baptist Bible' that you used to read in at school. I hope it will make a little Baptist of you some day, sure enough. You know that we girls treated you rudely about your little Baptist Bible, as you called it, but we were all ashamed of it afterwards. But, Mellie, I believe it turned out to make me a better girl after all. I really never knew how mean I was till that day Mr. Hamilton gave us that lecture about doing good for evil, and heaping coals of fire on the heads of our enemies. It seemed like every word went to my heart; and when I reflected about treating you so badly, and how kind you were to me in return, it was indeed coals of fire on my head, or something worse about my heart."

"Well, but our hearts melted and ran together, you remember, and we made it all up, and never cared for it any more," said Mellie, laughingly.

"Yes, we made it all up," said Laura, "but then, I felt so mean about it that I could not rest. I felt so unworthy that I didn't want anybody to see me. I went home and read my Bible, and prayed God to forgive me. I couldn't study my lessons in school, and when out of school I felt worse and worse. I was so justly condemned that I thought it would be right should God refuse His mercy to me, for I was such a sinner. But I just determined to pray as long as I lived, and if God sent me to torment, I would go praying. I then realized that I had nothing to depend on but the Saviour, and when I let go all other hopes and put my trust in Him, my burden of guilt seemed all at once to roll off, and I felt so happy that I could not help praising the Lord. All was then so quiet; and I experienced for myself the great peace there is in believing in Christ."

"And that's what made you be baptized, was it?" said Mellie. "I saw you, and you did look so happy. I told mamma I guessed that it was because you were obeying the Saviour that made you feel so good."

"Yes, Mellie," said Laura; "I found peace in believing on Him, and I find comfort and joy in obeying Him. Since He was so good as to save me, I want to serve Him all my life, and do all that I can for His cause."

"And you intend to do just what the Bible tells you, don't you?" asked Mellie.

"Yes," said Laura; "the Bible is the place for us to learn our duty. But, Mellie, I want you to be religious, and to be a follower of Christ too. You have always been a good girl—much better than myself—yet you cannot go where Jesus and the angels are unless you have a new heart. You must be born again. You have read in your little Bible that you must repent and be converted that your sins may be blotted out."

"I always try to be good, and I'm going to continue trying," said Mellie.

"Yes," said Laura, "I know that you do try to be good and to do right, but you must seek for God's grace to enable you to be good, and to prepare you for happiness, both here and hereafter. Don't you remember the lesson we had in school one day about the Publican and Pharisee?"

"O, yes," said Mellie, "I remember how Mr. Hamilton explained it. He told us not to be like the Pharisee, and think that we were better than others, but to be humble, like the poor Publican. I remember, too, that the Saviour said: 'He that humbleth himself shall be exalted, and he that exalteth himself shall be abased.' I will try to do all that the Bible tells me, Laura, and if I do that, that is all that is required, is it not?"

"Yes, that will do," said Laura, "but you must remember that the first duty enjoined upon you is to repent of your sins. If you are saved it must be by 'repentance toward God and faith toward the Lord Jesus Christ.' Take care, Mellie, that you do not become a little Pharisee, depending on your own goodness to save you. Remember you must deny yourself and trust in Christ. You must rely upon His merits, and not your own. It is because we cannot be saved by the Law, which requires a holy life, and perfect obedience, that Christ came to save us."

Mellie did not *feel* the truth of these things, yet she did not treat them lightly, nor forget them. Impressions were made on her mind that were never erased. Laura had sown seeds of truth into good ground that in process of time brought forth the desired fruit.

CHAPTER. X

THE COUNTRY SCHOOL—MRS. BROWN'S MENTAL AGITATIONS.

SOON after Mellie was fourteen years old, she was sent off to a select boarding school in the country, and placed under the care of one of her mother's particular friends—a lady of much experience as a teacher. She was gratified at this arrangement; for she not only loved to attend school and study, but she was delighted with life in the country, where she had opportunities of observing nature in all its varied phases. The following letter written to her mother, gives some idea of her situation, and the state of her mind:

"MY DEAR MAMMA:—I have now been at Forest Hill Seminary a little more than six months, and, as I have written to you before, my teacher is very kind to me, and shows me all the attention that I could desire. We have a nice and interesting school. The most of the students are young ladies, and though some of them are not much older than myself, they are much larger, and, as you may reasonably suppose, I am, as usual, called *little Mellie* Brown. They have not learned to call me the little Baptist yet, and upon that subject we have no controversy. My class and roommates are the best girls that I ever saw.

Some of them are farther advanced than myself, and they assist me very much in learning my lessons. I wondered how so many girls, so nice and good, could have gotten together, but the teacher told me that the reason was she would not have any other kind in her school; that all had to come were commended, and then they must obey her rules and demean themselves properly, else she would not keep them. It is a good school, and no bad influences can find admittance here. I am so glad that papa sent me here, and I am trying to do all that I can to be a good scholar when I quit school. Two years will be a long time to stay away from home, but then I want to be good and wise, and I'll study hard and think as little about the two long years as possible. Papa will come for me in vacation and take me home for a few weeks, and that will be a happy time.

"I could tell you much about our rambles in the woods, and what fine times we have every day, but that would make my letter too long. I make it a rule to read some in my Bible every day, for I wish to learn how to be good, and I think the Bible is the book from which to learn my duty to God. I attend church every Sunday, and listen closely to all that the preacher says; and sometimes I feel like I am not good after all my efforts to be so. I fear that my heart is not right in the sight of God. Laura Thompson once told me that I must have a new heart before I would be prepared to associate with the blessed in Heaven, and I have been thinking a great deal about it of late. I never intended to be a sinner, but my Bible tells me that 'the heart is deceitful above all things, and desperately wicked.' And then it says so much about all being condemned under the law, and about God's people having new hearts given them, and having the Spirit to bear witness with theirs that they are the children of God. I know that I have had no experience of these things, and I am afraid that I am not so good as I thought I was. I know that if I am a sinner God is angry with me every day, for the Bible says so.

"Please write to me, mamma, and instruct me, for I feel as if I were wandering in darkness. Had you talked to me like Laura Thompson did, maybe I could have understood it all better. I can always understand what you say. But I will read and pray and try to find the right way. Mamma, write to me, and pray for

"Your affectionate daughter, MELLIE."

Mrs. Brown was glad to hear that Mellie was satisfied and doing well at school, but the latter part of her letter caused feelings of deep emotion. The question pressed heavily upon her mind: Had she done her duty? She had instructed Mellie in almost everything except the "one thing needful." On reviewing the past, she was forced to decide that the kind of training she had given her was liable to make her a strict Pharisee, and nothing more. She had failed to correct an error which seemed prominent in Mellie's mind: that she had only to be good—to be consistent in her morals, and Heaven would be given her as a reward of merit. She had not taught her that her heart was depraved by nature, and must be renewed by the Holy Spirit. Not one word had she ever told her about the necessity of repentance and faith, or of the necessity of obtaining a new heart to prepare her for entering the kingdom of Heaven. These facts caused her some sore reflections. She had had her children baptized in their infancy, according to the usage of her church, and in spite of her better informed judgment, and her understanding of the Scriptures, she gave a kind of tacit consent that there was some efficacy attached to it. The creed of her church, and the creeds of other Pedobaptist churches did, indirectly, at least teach that there was some sort of saving efficacy in baptism, and that children received virtue from the ordinance, that they were thereby brought into a "covenant relation with God." It is true, as she had intelligence enough to know, that the Pedobaptist denominations, generally, have outgrown their creeds; that they neither preach nor profess now what their creeds really teach upon this subject. But while they incorporate in their Confessions of Faith, and Articles of Religion, the exploded theories of past ages, they must, in some respects, be held responsible for the evils arising from misconstructions. If they would be fully and unmistakably understood to believe no more than they publicly teach, they must expunge from their creeds, every expression seeming to teach gross heresy of baptismal regeneration. Creeds, as well as sermons should teach individual responsibility and personal obedience, as well as personal faith. Then there need be no misunderstanding of terms.

No one who reads the Bible, divested of prejudice, and allows that it says what it means, and means what it says, can fail to see that all are condemned by the law of God. And to be saved by the law, would require a perfect and sinless obedience. "For whosoever shall keep the whole law, and yet offend in one point, he is guilty of all."—*James* 2:10.

A purity equal to the demands of God's law, cannot be attained by depraved beings. The coming of Christ as a mediator between God and man, and His fulfillment of the law in man's stead, is positive proof of man's inability to meet its demands. The fact that Christ died to make an atonement for sin, is proof that the atonement must be applied *personally*, and its healing effects realized. It avails nothing, that there is a remedy for a disease, if that remedy is never applied. But if the remedy is applied, one thing more is essential to establish its value—its healing effects must be experimentally realized. Then, to sum it up: natural depravity is the disease; the blood of Christ is the remedy; the Holy Spirit must make the application, and experimental consciousness of the effects must be felt and known.

Mrs. Brown felt that she knew something of experimental religion. The time when she realized the full pardon of her sins could never be erased from her mind. She knew the meaning of the expressions: "born from above," "brought from darkness to light," "created anew," but her conscience was not at ease, because she had failed to direct the minds of her children to a realization of the fact that they, too, must be "renewed in heart," as a preparation to meet God in peace. She had been teaching them to be Christians, without first teaching them that they were sinners—a very fatal mistake. But what now should she do? She would write to Mellie at once. And she did write to her, to "read her Bible, and pray God to enlighten her mind so that she might feel the full need of repentance." "You have ever been a good child," said her mother, "yet you are by nature sinful, and a child of wrath, even as others. As much as you have been praised for being good, you are yet bad—sinful, and a sinner in the sight of God, and in need of being cleansed by the blood of Christ. Pray, my dear child, that God, for Christ's sake, may pardon your sins and renew your heart, so that you may realize His love in all its fullness. Don't conclude for a moment; that you are better than others, but remember that you are just the character that Christ calls on to repent. Think not that because you were reared up in the church as a baptized member, that this will avail you anything in the great day of accounts. No doubt I have wronged you by not impressing these truths on your mind before this, but the best amend I can now make, is to warn you faithfully and entreat you earnestly, to seek the Lord while He may be found, and call upon Him while He is near. You have long ago decided for yourself that your baptism has secured you *nothing at all*; and, let me assure you that your morality and good deeds, while most worthy and commendable, and well pleasing in the sight of God, are not sufficient to secure the salvation of your soul. You are too young to have much actual transgression laid to your charge, but you are old enough—enlightened enough, to know good from evil, therefore you are old enough for God to judge you and hold you accountable. You will be judged not according to age, but according to your knowledge of your duty. You have no doubt, often read in your Bible, that those who know the Master's will and do it not, shall be beaten with many stripes. I hope, my dear, to soon hear that God has led you out from the dark shadows of unbelief into the bright morning of His love; that you have found your way to the cross of Christ, and realized a happy peace to your soul. If you feel that you are a sinner, and are honestly seeking deliverance, all the promises of the Bible are yours. Venture on the Saviour, and trust Him for His grace, for He has never sent one away who sought Him with the whole heart. Whosoever will, may partake of the Water of Life freely."

CHAPTER XI.

BAPTISMAL REGENERATION MELLIE'S CONVERSION.

AFTER graduating with high honors, Frank Brown returned from College and commenced the practice of law. As regards outward forms, he was a Presbyterian of the strictest fashion. He was punctual to attend church; contributed liberally to the support of his pastor; and duly observed the Sabbath. Moral and chaste in all his deportment, he was esteemed a model young man. He had great faith in the church and its ordinances, but to the effects of saving grace on the heart, he was wholly a stranger, as will hereafter appear. He was learned in the sciences taught in the schools, but the science of Christianity he had never studied. He had often heard it repeated that baptism places the child within the "covenant of grace," and he doubted not that there was a good reason for such expressions, hence the appeals from the pulpit to "repent and turn to God," were by him unheeded. That he was under obligations to render a personal obedience to the requirements of the gospel, was a thing he had not considered. Mellie's letter, and his mother's reply, attracted his attention with peculiar force, and he said:

"Mother, why did you have us all baptized if it

is true, as you wrote to sister, that it does us no good, and leaves us 'children of wrath, even as others' who have never had this advantage—if advantage it be?"

"Because," said Mrs. Brown, "the customs and rules of the church require it. I don't know any other reason. I never questioned that it was right, still I can't see any good it does." "Well, if there is no good to arise from it," said Frank, "I don't see any use there is for the practice. It is plainly taught in the Catechism and Confession of Faith, as well as many other books that I have read, as a positive duty; but, then, if it don't do children any good to baptize them, it is all a piece of hum buggery—just calculated to deceive children. If baptized children are not Christians, not regenerated, and have no advantage of unbaptized children, common sense teaches me that they ought not to be in the church."

"My son," said his mother, "I cannot dispute your reasoning. I have been thinking much on this subject of late. I intend to give it a further examination in the light of God's truth, and see if I can find any authority for the practice. The gospel is, of course, addressed to us personally. Each individual must hear, believe and obey for himself. I am fully satisfied that the baptism of a child on the faith of its parents, is not the act of the child, nor can it possibly be transferred so as to answer for the child's obedience. No act of a parent can release the child from obligation to obey the commands of Christ whenever it reaches a stage of accountability. Repentance, faith and baptism, are alike personal duties, which cannot be performed by another."

"Well, mother, that is strange talk to come from one who has always been considered such a reliable and devoted Presbyterian, and has been so much interested in having her children brought up in the same fold. Surely, little sister has turned you to a Baptist too,"

"It is true, Frank, that Mellie did put me to thinking; and thinking and reading together, have gone far toward settling me in the Baptist faith. It has caused me to doubt much that once I accepted as true, just because other people said it was so. I am yet undecided as to what course to pursue, but the more I investigate the subject, the more doubts I have relative to the Bible authority for my baptism, and for infant baptism too. I do think, too, that there is a growing disposition among too many of the different denominations, and with our church less than others, to, in a good degree, ignore experimental religion. They make it too much of mental training—place too much stress on educating the young to Christianity."

"Surely, mother, said Frank, "the better educated people are, the better Christians they will make, for

'If ignorance is bless,
'Tis folly to be wise' "

"Very true, my son," continued Mrs. Brown; "the more education the better, if it be rightly used; but, I mean, that there is with some a reliance on it for salvation. There is a tendency to teach children to be Christians, when they should be taught that *they are sinners*, in need of regenerating grace. True religion consists not in mental training, but in a change of heart, and this can only be effected by the power of the Holy Spirit. The Saviour said: 'They shall all be taught of God.' Our moral nature is depraved, and something more than education is required to purify it. All the mental culture in the world cannot renew the heart of the sinner. So far as it enlightens the judgment, enabling the sinner to realize the necessity of regeneration, it comes in as a valuable acquisition; but if it tends not to humility, there is danger of its proving a curse. For while education increases our responsibility, it cannot discover a new way to Heaven; for 'strait is the gate, and narrow is the way that leadeth unto life.' The wise, as well as the ignorant, must humbly trust in Christ, who is the only name given whereby we may be saved. And it is said that 'the wisdom of men is foolishness with God,' and that there are some things that God has hidden from the wise, and yet revealed unto babes.

Several days had passed since the last conversation, when Frank came into his mother's room and said: "Now, mother, I want to show you that there is a virtue in the baptism of infants, else our church, and all the other churches that practice it, are wrong. How could so many good and wise men be mistaken, and why should they teach that baptism regenerates the child, if it is not so?"

"You are mistaken, Frank," said his mother; "*our* church does not teach baptismal regeneration, nor any of the other churches, as far as I know. They don't baptize children to make them Christians."

"No, mother, I am not mistaken; I have the *documents* on it, as the lawyers say. Here is the Episcopalians' 'Book of Common Prayer,' and in the formula for the baptism of infants, after baptism, the minister says: 'Seeing now that *this child* is regenerated and grafted into the holy body of Christ's church, let us give thanks unto Almighty God for these benefits, and with one accord make our prayers unto Him, that *this child* may lead the rest of his life according to this beginning.' Again: 'We yield Thee hearty thanks, most merciful Father, that it has pleased Thee to regenerate this infant with Thy Holy Spirit, to receive him for Thine own child by adoption, and to incorporate him into Thy Holy church.' This is on page 220; and then on page 234, in the Catechism, they say: 'There are two sacraments necessary to salvation—that is to say, Baptism and the Lord's Supper.' Then they say again: 'There are two parts to a sacrament the outward visible sign, and the inward spiritual grace.' In baptism, 'water is the outward visible sign,' and 'a death unto sin, and a new birth unto righteousness,' the invisible sign. 'For being by nature born in sin, and the children of wrath, we are hereby (by baptism) made the children of grace."

"Do the Episcopalians teach *that* doctrine?" asked Mrs. Brown, with a look of surprise.

"Yes, indeed they do," said Frank, "and that's not all. Here is the Methodists' Discipline, and on page 27, edition 1859, it reads: 'Baptism is not only a sign of profession, and mark of difference whereby Christians are distinguished from others that are not baptized, but it is the sign of regeneration, or the new birth.' Baptism is also called a sacrament, and a sacrament is defined to be 'a certain sign of God's good will toward us, by the which He doth work invisibly in us, and doth not only quicken, but also strengthen and confirm our faith in Him'—page 26. In the formula, the minister prays to God to 'grant that *this child* now about to be baptized, may receive the fullness of Thy grace, and ever remain in the number of Thy faithful and elect children.' Now, if there is not *a little* baptismal regeneration in this, I must confess that I do not understand the right use of language."

"Well, well—perhaps they have some way of explaining it differently," remarked Mrs. Brown.

"Well, but, mother," replied Frank, "they have no right to explain it differently. They have put it in the book, in plain language, and they have no right to explain it away. If they meant something else, they should have put something else in the book, and have said exactly what they meant. Besides, if it is not the truth, its standing in the book is liable to do great harm, because they can't always have somebody present when the book is being read, to give the explanation, and children, whether they are regenerated or not, are liable to believe that such was intended by their baptism. But now let us take up our own old, and time honored Confession of Faith, and see what '*we* Presbyterians' think about it. On page 145, the book says: 'Sacraments are holy signs and seals of the covenant of grace.' *Signs and seals*—please notice that, mother! On page 148, it says: 'Baptism is a sacrament of the New Testament, ordained by Jesus Christ, not only for the solemn admission of the party baptized into the visible church, but also to be unto him a sign and seal of the covenant of grace, of his ingrafting into Christ, of regeneration, of remission of sins,' etc. *Sign and seal* again, mother! Then, on page 340, it says further: 'The parts of a sacrament are two; the one, an outward and sensible sign, used according to Christ's own appointment; the other, an inward and spiritual grace thereby signified.' A *sign* which *signifies inward grace*, notice if you please. Now, is not this strong language, and to the point too? And with these declarations standing in *our* book of *faith,* how are we to escape the charge of believing in baptismal regeneration? To view the language in the most liberal sense, baptism is an outward and sensible sign of an inward and spiritual grace. The child baptized has this grace before baptism, or gains possession of it in baptism. If not, the sign bears false testimony. Has not sister the sign signifying grace within? And did you not have the sign placed here? The question now is, has she the grace signified? If not, the sign placed upon her in the solemn name of the Trinity, testifies to that which is false. I know you did not intend for this solemn service to bear false testimony, and the preacher certainly knew what he was doing. So I conclude that the doctrine must be true; for our preachers are all learned men, and know much more than I do about the Bible."

Mrs. Brown was thoroughly confused, but she ventured at last to say: "I don't believe that baptism or any outward ceremony confers or seals any spiritual grace, and therefore, I see no reason for baptizing children before they are capable of understanding and acting for themselves. I can find no Bible authority, nor even a reasonable excuse for it. Still I do not charge my church with believing in baptismal regeneration. The old Fathers may have done so long ago, when the church was just merging out of the dark ages of ignorance and superstition, but our people have outgrown that now; they don't preach it, and I presume they do not understand the book to teach that anyone is saved by baptism."

"Maybe not *by* baptism," said Frank, "but *on account of*, or *in consideration* of baptism, the Holy Spirit regenerates the child. I read on page 152, that 'The efficacy of baptism is not tied to that moment of time when it is administered, yet, notwithstanding, by the right use of this ordinance, the grace promised is not only offered, but really exhibited and conferred by the Holy

Ghost to such (whether of age or infants) as that grace belongeth unto, according to the counsels of God's own will, in His appointed time.' And I am sure, mother, that our church takes it for granted that all the baptized children are regenerated, or *will be,* for on page 461, the rule is, 'All baptized persons are members of the church, are under its care, and subject to its government and discipline; and when they have arrived at the years of discretion, they are bound to perform all the duties of church members.'"

Mrs. Brown took the book and read on page 151: "Although it be a great sin to contemn or neglect this ordinance, yet grace and salvation are not so inseparably annexed unto it as that no person can be regenerated and saved without it, or that all that are baptized are undoubtedly regenerated."

She asked Frank to go into the library and bring Dick's Lectures on Theology, which she knew to be a standard work in her church, and whatever it taught might be regarded as orthodox Presbyterianism. While he was gone she pondered the question: is grace in any way connected with baptism? The book was brought, and she opened it, and on page 475 read: "Baptism being a Divine institution, no adult person can safely neglect it; yet it is not so connected with salvation that unbaptized children are excluded from the kingdom of Heaven. We cannot persuade ourselves that the salvation of infants is so much in the power of their parents that they can deprive them of eternal life, by their carelessness or deliberate wickedness. Baptism is only a sign of the communication of spiritual blessings; and we entertain, no doubt, that as the sign is not always accompanied with the thing signified, so the thing signified is often enjoyed without the sign."

Frank interrupted the reading by saying: "Well, mother, I think that is strange reasoning to come from a great man like Dr. Dick. He seems to argue that baptism is somehow connected with the conferring of grace, and a very important thing; yet the 'carelessness or deliberate wickedness' or the parents will insure the salvation of the child just as well. Oh, for the jewel of consistency!"

Mrs. Brown continued to read: "We do not with some Baptists and too many Protestants, and particularly with some half-popish Divines of the Church of England, hold the strange unscriptural opinion, which is too much countenanced by the language of their liturgy, that baptism is regeneration... We are convinced that there is a baptism of the Spirit, distinct from the baptism of water; that the former does not always accompany the latter; and that God gives the Spirit to whom He pleases, without limiting the gift to the usage of the sign." "This," said Mrs. Brown, "I think is sensible."

"Sensible, it may be," said Frank, "but who can tell after all what is really the doctrine of the Presbyterian church on this subject? Baptismal regeneration is taught in one place and contradicted in another; and while Dr. Dick holds on the one hand that it is efficacious in conferring and signifying grace, on the other he admits that God gives the Spirit to whom He will, independent of baptism. If the Pedobaptist churches do not mean to teach that infants are regenerated by baptism, they ought to change the language of their creeds and rituals, for there is danger of thousands of children being deceived, as I was by reading them. Why don't they have their books to say what they mean, and to mean what they say? For surely no good can come of mystifying a plain subject; and if it is true that the churches have outgrown their creeds, why don't they make new ones, else fall back on the Bible?"

Mrs. Brown was called away to attend to some domestic duties, and the conversation here ended.

* * * * * * * * * * * *

Time, which never waits for mortals, has been rolling on. Mellie Brown has been home and spent her vacation, but returned again to school. It was near the close of her second year, she wrote the following letter:

"MY DEAR MOTHER:—I received your kind letter last week, which I found exceedingly interesting. As the session nears its close, I become more and more anxious to go home. I am wearied with study, and feel that my mind needs rest. I cannot relax my efforts now, for I am determined to do my best to be equal to any at the examination, so that if Papa and Buddie come they will have no cause to be ashamed of me. But there is one thing that I must tell you:

I have at last found the 'pearl of great price;' I feel that I am in truth a new creature! Old things have passed away, and all things have become new. I now realize what it is to have the love of Christ in my soul, and feel His spirit bearing witness with mine that I am born from above, and adopted an heir of Heaven. The Bible says: 'We know that we have passed from death unto life because we love the brethren,' and I feel like I love everybody. I long to see you, that I may tell you all about it, and to get you to help me praise the Lord for His goodness. I can say, with David, 'Bless the Lord, O, my soul,' and with Job, 'I know that my Redeemer liveth.' Mamma, I feel so happy that I can scarcely be still while I write.

"You know that when I was at home, I told you that I wanted to know for myself what it was to have the love of God in my soul, and you told me so many things which I never until now could understand. I see now that instead of being a believer in the Saviour before, I was only a self-righteous Pharisee, trusting in my own good deeds to save me. I was not depending on Christ to save me, a sinner on account of His blood, but for my goodness. I thought I was good, and I was proud and vain enough to love to be praised for it. How like the proud Pharisee who loved the praise of men more than the praise of God! But I thought that God would be sure to save *me* anyhow. I remember that before I read my Bible, I thought that as I was a baptized child and in the church, I had nothing to fear; that all the calls to repentance were intended for others who were aliens from God and out of the church; but as I became older and read the Bible more, and understood it better, I found myself to be a vile sinner. Then I made another mistake just as bad, for I thought I would get very good, and that God would reward me with His favor. So I undertook to keep the law and be perfect in all my thoughts and actions; but I soon learned that this would not do. Now I see there was sin in the very thought. It was nothing less than base presumption in me, and was treating my Saviour with contempt to be trying to save myself after He had died to save me. After I had tried all other means and failed, I humbly prostrated myself at the foot of the cross, fully realizing that I was a justly condemned sinner, destitute of all merit of my own, and wholly dependent on God's mercy through Christ. I realized my helpless condition, and was anxious to be saved upon God's own terms—upon any terms, I could only say:

'Nothing in my hands I bring,
Simply to Thy cross I cling.'

"For the first time in my life, I could say: 'Not my will, O Lord, but Thine be done;' and just the moment that I surrendered every other hope, and fully trusted in the Lord, He spoke peace to my soul. I felt calm and delightful. My troubles were instantly gone, and all that was within me praised the Lord. Why, mamma, there was no miracle in this, not even a mystery in the *fact*. We know not how it is done, any more than we know how the wind blows, yet we know the effect, and it is no delusion. It is just as the Saviour promised: 'Come unto me, and I will give you rest.' Whenever we deny ourselves and trust in Christ, He is ready and willing to receive us, but He has never promised to receive us while we are trusting in ourselves or in something else. The way now looks so easy that it seems like I could tell everybody how to be Christians. Why, it's so plain—just to deny ourselves and *look* to Jesus. I had only to quit trying to save myself and be willing for the Lord to save me—that was all; and He will save every one, *if they will only be willing.*

"I intend, after getting home, to try to obey my Saviour by walking in obedience to all His commandments. He has said: 'If ye love me, keep my commandments;' and as an evidence of my love to Him, I will take up my cross and follow Him. Let the world say what it may,

'I'm not ashamed to own my Lord,
  Nor to defend His cause;
Maintain the honor of His word,
  The glory of His cross.'

"When I see you, I will have much more to tell you. Remember me in your prayers.
"Your affectionate daughter,
"MELLIE."

CHAPTER XII.

DISCUSSION OF BAPTISM.

Mellie is again at home with her mother. Seven years of her life have gone by since she was first introduced to the reader. She has grown much; and observation, experience and education, have done for her all that could have been done for any one under like circumstances. She is yet small, though now a young lady, and her intelligence is such, that she is peculiarly attractive. Her acquaintances still speak of her as "Little Mellie;" and the little "Baptist Bible," though greatly damaged by use, is still preserved. She has read, and reread, until she is familiar with its teachings; and pencil marks, designating noted texts, are found on many of its pages. She remains true to her first impression that it is a Baptist book; and she intends that it shall not be long until it will be no mistake when her friends call her the "Little Baptist." Having taken proper time to deliberate, she is now resolved to act. She desires to obey her Saviour, by her own voluntary action, in the ordinances of His church. She no longer looks specially and solely to "the recompense of reward," but is moved by a sense of duty. She recognizes the right of Christ to command, and the duty of His followers to obey. In the Bible she finds the path of duty plainly marked out. She having believed, intends soon to be baptized, emblematically showing her faith in a buried and risen Saviour. It was something of a trial for her to leave the church in which she had been *nominally* a member, and in which her relatives for several generations had lived and died; yet she calmly counted the cost, decided upon her course, and moved steadily forward. Her mother, having adopted her views, of course became a tower of strength to her, though so firm was her faith, that had she been left to act alone, she would have done what she felt that her Saviour required of her. Mellie and Frank had often tried their skill at argument; and, in many well contested conflicts, Mellie had held her ground nobly and triumphantly. This was, in part, because she knew more of the Bible than Frank, but more especially because the Bible favored her side of the question.

Frank, with all his virtues, had acquired some very aristocratic notions. He had much pride, and looked forward with ambitious hopes to fame and popular applause. A partiality for the Presbyterian church was early instilled into him, and he had a denominational pride that made him jealous of its fame. And, too, a majority of the most wealthy people of the community belonged to this church, or were under its influence; this, to one who felt himself to be a "rising man," was a natural stimulant to him to keep "fair weather" in that direction. He determined that, if possible, he would prevent his mother and Mellie from leaving their church.

He had tried in every way to dissuade them from the too free expression of their opinions; which he saw was destined to bring trouble on the church, and afford gossip for the whole community. But finding them determined and immovable, he resorted to the strategy of having Dr. Farnsworth to casually call to spend the day with them. Frank hoped that the Doctor, by his great learning and powers of argument, might succeed in influencing them to change their purpose; not reflecting that God sometimes chooses the weak to confound the mighty, and the foolish to confound the wise.

Early on Monday morning, Dr. Farnsworth called at Col. Brown's to make a last effort to reclaim his "erring members," as he had frequently called Mrs. Brown and Mellie. He was somewhat encouraged by seeing them in their accustomed seats the day previous, and especially as he discovered no change in the countenance of either of them when he made some heavy thrusts at the "heresies of the times"— a few remarks that had been well prepared for a special object, but which were, seemingly, only casually thrown into the discourse.

As soon as it appeared polite to do so, Dr. Farnsworth accosted Mellie in a kind of flattering manner, relative to the improvement made on her by the country school, and being little disposed to waste time in ceremonies, he said:

"How is it, Mellie, that you, being so small, are attracting so much attention in the community?

It appears that *your person*, and *your opinions* are monopolizing the attention of the whole town."

Mellie blushed, and for an instant seemed overcome with diffidence, but on regaining her composure, she replied. "I think the compliment must be overdrawn, Doctor. If my person is attractive, I do not know why, unless people think the old saying true, that 'valuable articles are always put up in small packages;' and, as regards my opinions, I cannot suppose they are entitled to any great attention. Please enlighten me further as to your meaning, Doctor."

Somewhat at a loss for words leading him in the right direction, the Doctor said: "Well, Mellie, you are reported to have some very strange ideas for a Presbyterian, especially, on the subject of baptism, and I wish to have a candid talk with you for the purpose of trying to correct your errors. I, as your pastor, have felt it my duty to seek this interview with you, which liberty I hope you will not construe into an offense."

"By no means," replied Mellie, "I thank you for the interest manifested, and will gladly hear all that you may wish to say. I assure you that I only desire to know the truth. I would rather be a Presbyterian than not if I could feel sure that the Bible sustained their views. I want the Bible to be my guide, and intend to try to go where it leads me."

"Well, the *truth*, Mellie, is, that you were baptized in your infancy, and you should be satisfied with *that*, and give the subject no further attention," said the Doctor, in a rather impatient manner.

"But, Doctor," said Mellie, "my baptism in infancy was no act of mine, and Christ commands *me* to be baptized. I have recently become a believer in Christ, and I find that He has laid down my duty in plain language, and requires of me obedience. I, as you know, was wholly unconscious of what my parents did for me in my infancy, and now I cannot make it *my* act of obedience. For, if I understand the Bible, it teaches that all obedience must be personal and voluntary, else it is not acceptable."

The Doctor very gravely replied: "Have you never reflected on what a solemn thing it is for you to call in question what your parents did for you in placing you within the covenant of grace, whereby you were received among God's elect children and accepted a member of his church?"

"Dr. Farnsworth," said Mellie, "please take the Bible and show me where my parents are commanded to have their children baptized; that will settle the controversy, and reclaim me at once from my errors, if I am in error."

The Doctor was sensible of his situation, but to make a fair appearance, he must do something, so he said: "Some things are not expressed, but merely implied; and there are some things that must be drawn from inference."

"Is the duty to baptize believers, a command or an inference?" asked Mellie. "Clearly a command—that is, provided they have not been baptized in infancy," answered the Doctor.

"But where is this exception found Doctor?" said Mellie. "What I want to see is a command to baptize infants."

Contrary to his expectations, the Doctor was entrapped, and his courage faltered. To be asked to show a command for the baptism of infants, when he well knew that the Bible did not contain one word on the subject, was placing him in a position that sorely puzzled him. Yet he looked as wise as he could while turning the Bible, and finally read that noted text, "Suffer little children to come unto me and forbid them not, for of such is the kingdom of heaven."

To this Mellie replied: "Yes; I have read that many times, and can't see even an *inference* that He baptized them. Now, they brought the children to Christ, we will accept this as a *fact*; then the question is, *what did Christ do?* The Bible tells plainly what He did; He *took them in His arms*; He *laid His hands on them*; then, He *blessed them*—that is all, and we have no right to infer anything more. If He baptized them, why does not the Bible say so? Christ said to His disciples: 'Except ye repent and become as little children, ye shall not enter into the kingdom of heaven.' In this text, Christ was endeavoring to teach a lesson of humility—that they should be innocent, humble and dependent. There is no baptism in this; but, Doctor, if there is anywhere in the Bible, a command to baptize infants, surely you can find it."

Dr. Farnsworth then remarked: "I suppose you have read of the jailor and his household; of

Lydia and her household, and of Stephanas and his house all being baptized. And, of course, among so many household baptisms, there must have been children. We should infer that there were children in some of them, at least."

"But," said Mellie, "is it not just as easy to infer that there *were not* any children? It would be as reasonable, and I think much safer, to only believe what the Bible says, and no more. Suppose you were a stranger in town, and some one should tell you that Esquire Thompson and his household were baptized, or that Mr. Morris and his house were baptized, you might infer that some infants were baptized, as a matter of course, but you see this would be a mistake, because in one, the children are all grown, and in the other, there never were any children. And if you will look into the different households in town, you will find that about one half contain no infants. As regards the jailer's house, whoever may have been the members of it, it is certain that they were not infants, for they all *believed* and *rejoiced* together. And as to Lydia, it is stretching the inference rather far, it seems to me, to say that she had infant children. But the Bible settles this, leaving no room for inference. For when Paul and Silas returned again to the house of Lydia, they 'comforted the brethren;' so, whatever they were, they were called 'brethren,' and, therefore were not infants."

"O, yes," said the Doctor, "I see that you have the Baptist argument very well. I must confess that you are an apt scholar. But you have never yet realized the *gist* of the question. What ought to satisfy you, or anyone else, is the inference to be drawn from the law of circumcision, which was instituted in the family of Abraham. And because baptism has come in the place of circumcision, children ought to be baptized just as they were required to be circumcised."

"But, Doctor," said Mellie, "I am governed by my Bible; will you please enlighten me by showing the passage which says that baptism came in the place of circumcision? I have heard that asserted so often, yet after searching the Bible through, I have failed to find it." "I do not pretend to say," said he, "that it is there at all, just in so many words, but that is the inference drawn from various expressions and circumstances."

Mrs. Brown had preserved silence from the first, and intended not to interfere in the conversation, but after Dr. Farnsworth had failed to point out any Scripture bearing directly upon the subject at issue, her patience became exhausted, and she exclaimed: "Inference! I hoped you could give us some reason if not scripture, for the practice of infant baptism. If the whole theory hangs on inference, why not tell the people so plainly?"

The Doctor stepped for a drink of water, and Mellie asked him: "To whom was the law of circumcision given?"

"To the Jews, through Abraham," said he.

"Well, then, to whom was the law of baptism given?"

"The law of baptism was given to the disciples,

or, I might say, to Christians."

"I do not wish to be impertinent," said Mellie, "but let me inquire if the Jews did not strictly obey the law of circumcision?"

"They did, most scrupulously so, and do to this day," said he.

"Then, Doctor, ought not Christians to be content with obeying the law given especially to them, without going to the Jews to borrow a part of their rites?"

As the Doctor was slow framing an answer to the last question, Mrs. Brown remarked: "For my part, I don't believe that God has left any duty to be learned from mere inference. The Jews had a plain law; they understood it and obeyed it. Christians have the law of baptism as plain as language can make it, therefore they ought to observe it."

"Yes," said Mellie, "God wanted believers to be baptized, and He told us so. He did not tell us to baptize infants, therefore it is safe to infer that He did not want us to do that."

Dr. Farnsworth referred, at some length, to the "customs of the church," and to the "writings of the Fathers," and told what many men of piety and distinguished ability had said and written upon the subject, and began to quote extensively from ecclesiastical history, but Mellie stopped him by replying that she only proposed to inquire what the Bible said; that she had determined to take the Bible for her guide, and would not be influenced by what the history of the past might teach, or by the opinions of fallible men; that the

Bible should govern her faith, and be the rule of her actions; she would obey what she could understand, and any duty not plainly revealed, she was sure God did not require of her. She said: "I can understand the duty of all believers to be baptized, but I cannot understand how anything done for them by their parents, can excuse them from personal obedience. And no one can obey a command without faith, 'for whatsoever is not of faith is sin.'"

"I acknowledge that you are a close reasoner, Mellie," said Dr. Farnsworth; "but you and I look at things from very different standpoints. I yet hope that you may see your error, and not be led off from the church in which you have been dedicated to God. Don't you think that your course is showing a want of respect for your parents, and treating the church even with disrespect?"

"Let it be so," said Mrs. Brown, a little more irritated than she ought to have been. "If the Scriptures don't authorize infant baptism, (and if they do you fail to discover it), let her obey Christ for herself. I intend that Mellie shall do as she believes her Bible teaches her is right. I have been a long time thinking about this subject myself, and since you fail to show the authority, I am fully satisfied that there is neither precept nor example for the practice of our church on the subject of baptism. I just consider that I have not been baptized myself, and the church, or the ministers, are to blame for it. I have followed the teachings of men without learing my duty as revealed in the Bible, and that is why this precept has been neglected."

Dr. Farnsworth took up his hat preparatory to leaving but Mellie entreated him to remain longer and answer her a few questions relative to the mode or action of baptism. To this he reluctantly assented, and told her to proceed with her questions.

"Don't you think that Christ was baptized by immersion?" asked Mellie.

The Doctor said: "I am not bound to admit that He was. It is possible, yet by no means certain. But grant that he was immersed in the river Jordan, as you and your Baptist friends contend, we are not in the least bound by that. Christian baptism was not instituted until the giving of the Commission; and you know that the baptism of John, that Christ received, has never been considered by our church as Christian baptism."

"Does not the term Christian mean Christ like?" asked Mellie "And what is Christian baptism if it is not to be baptized in the same manner that Christ himself was? He said to His disciples, 'follow me,' and I am sure that if we follow Him, we will never do an *un*christian act. Then did not Philip baptize the Eunuch after the giving of the Commission? It appears to me that the Commission neither introduced any new rite, nor change any old one. It enlarged the disciples' field of labor—nothing more. Prior to this, they had been restricted to the Jews; now they are told to go into all the world and preach the gospel to every creature—not to the Jews alone, now but go teach all nations, and whosoever believeth and is baptized, shall be saved."

Dr. Farnsworth referred again to the case of Philip and the Eunuch, and said: "Because they both went down into the water, it does not necessarily follow that there was an immersion; for on the day of Pentecost there were added to the disciples about three thousand souls, and were all baptized. This, you must know, could not have been done by immersion, because there was not time enough."

"But, Doctor," said Mellie, "pray tell me how much more time it takes to immerse than to sprinkle a person? As all of the apostles were there together, they could have divided them out, and immersed them in a short time. The apostles could easily have immersed 3,000 persons in four and a half hours. That is only one a minute. In India three Baptist preachers immersed 2,222 in 6 hours. Twelve could at that rate have immersed 8,888 in 6 hours. Some of them, however, may have waited until the next day or the next week, as the Bible does not say when they were baptized, only that they were added to the church that day. Could they not have made a profession of discipleship that day and have received baptism afterward? You will allow me to *infer* this, will you not?"

"Yes, yes," said the Doctor, "you can *infer* anything you please."

"So you will agree, Doctor that inference is an unsafe guide, I presume?"

"Not always—not necessarily so; but, Mellie, how do you fix it up about the baptism of the Holy Ghost, which was *poured* out upon the people? The people were immersed, were they?"

"I suppose," said Mellie, "that the influence of the Holy Spirit on this occasion was *overwhelming*, therefore figuratively called a baptism. The figure so well represents immersion, that it is appropriately called a baptism. Why not call this a baptism on account of its over-whelming, power, as well as for Christ to have called His sufferings a baptism? I suppose that when ministers pray for a baptism of the Holy Spirit, they mean an immersion—an overwhelming effect; they certainly don't mean *just a little*, like sprinkling."

"O, but," said the Doctor, "you forget that the Bible speaks of the pouring out of the Spirit, what does this mean?" "Well, it means, no doubt," said Mellie "just what you meant on yesterday, when in your sermon you became a little poetical, and spoke of the 'sun *pouring his rays* down on the earth on a July moon.' In both instances the speakers used figurative language, and the idea has reference to the *power* and *not* to the manner. You would never say the sun pours down his rays early in the morning, but you would say, 'The gentle beams of the rising sun,' as some poet has said; and young as I am, I have learned that there is a limit to the ideas in figures of speech and poetical allusions, as well as in other cases."

"Your imagination is very prolific, I find," said

the Doctor, "and I presume you can see that Christ was immersed on the cross because He referred to His sufferings as a baptism?"

"No," replied Mellie, "I *can't see* that He was immersed on the cross, nor *can I see* that He was either *poured* or *sprinkled* on the cross, but I *can see* that He was *overwhelmed* with sufferings. It is not uncommon to hear persons speak of being 'overwhelmed with sorrows,' or of being 'immersed in cares,' or 'immersed in business.' Such expressions may be heard frequently, but no one yet has so warped the figure as to say, 'poured with sorrows,' 'poured in cares,' or 'sprinkled in business.' Figures are strictly representative. Don't you remember that the hymn you used on yesterday begins,

'*Plunged* in a gulf of dark despair,
 We wretched sinners law,'

thus presenting an idea in figurative language that we readily comprehend. We know that by the word *plunged*, the poet meant *overwhelmed*; and another poet has described our condition by nature as being

'Overwhelmed in sin and sore distress.'

Then there is mamma's favorite hymn, beginning,

"There is a fountain filled with blood,
 Drawn from Immanuel's veins,
 And sinners *plunged* beneath that flood

Lose all their guilty stains.'

Such figures of speech are easily understood only when they occur in the Bible with reference to baptism."

"Since I have turned questioner," said Dr. Farnsworth, "let me inquire how were the people 'baptized unto Moses, in the cloud and in the sea?' The waters were divided, standing, on either side of the Israelites as they went through, there was also the cloud; and I wish to see how you avoid the conclusion that the spray from the sea, and a shower of rain from the cloud, sprinkled the people so as to be very appropriately termed a baptism."

"I take this as another figurative allusion," she said, "and not a literal fact. I do not read of any *spray* arising from the sea, whose waters stood *congealed* on either side; nor do I read of any cloud that was likely to have produced a shower of rain. My Bible describes a significance of the presence of the Almighty, appearing as a pillar of cloud by day, and a pillar of fire by night, to guide the Israelites in their journey, and assure them of His protection; but I cannot suppose that any person really believes that this pillar of cloud gave forth a shower of rain. This Bible says they went over dry shod. The allusion to baptism is only figurative, but if it could be construed into a literal baptism at all, it would be because the water formed a wall on either side, and the cloud covered them above, thus enveloping them. But the most reasonable interpretation, it occurs to me, is that the Israelites, going out of Egyptian bondage, and witnessing their miraculous salvation at the sea, in going through, acknowledged their allegiance to Moses as their leader and deliverer, just as a person by baptism renounces the bondage of Satan and professes allegiance to Christ. Hence the event is called a baptism unto Moses. Now you know, Doctor, that I take nothing as a proof in doctrine or practice except the Bible, but Dr. McKnight was a good Presbyterian, and as he understood it about as I have expressed it, he may be authority with you, so I will read what he says: 'And all were baptized into the belief of Moses' divine mission, by their being hidden from the Egyptians in the cloud, and by their passage through the sea miraculously.' And again he says: 'Because the Israelites, by being hid from the Egyptians under the cloud, and by passing through the Red Sea, were made to declare their belief in the Lord and His servant Moses, the apostle very properly represents them as being baptized unto Moses in the cloud and in the sea."

The Doctor had despaired of accomplishing the object of his visit; and being narrowed down to the Bible in the discussion, he, as a matter of course, could say but little. He had been interested in drawing out Mellie's opinions merely to see what arguments and explanations she was able to make in relation to the doctrine that she was advocating. After satisfying himself that she was fully posted in the Scriptures and would hear to nothing outside, he said: "Mellie, I see that you are determined to have your own way; therefore it is but a waste of time for me to reason with you. It is strange, yet, nevertheless true, that when any person imbibes Baptist sentiments, they become hardheaded and unteachable: they invariably fall back on the Bible, and you can't get them away from it. If you, Mellie, would only listen to me, I could produce history and the writings of the Fathers of the church, to show you clearly that sprinkling and pouring were most probably the original manner of administering baptism. But, if this is not so, the church has changed the mode, yet retained the same object, and our adopted practice does just as well, besides being much more convenient."

Mellie impatiently replied: "I don't care what history says, nor what the Fathers in the church have said, and it makes no difference to me how many times the church has changed Christ's ordinances, I am to be governed by what I understand the Bible to say, and, so far, you have declined to assume that the Bible says one word about infant baptism, and have given no proof that it favors sprinkling or pouring for baptism."

"I have repeatedly told you, Mellie," said he, "that it does not in so many words command the baptism of infants, yet I think that it indirectly teaches it, and according to history, it was practiced a few centuries after the days of the apostles."

"You are a Greek scholar, Doctor, and please to

candidly answer me one question: Does the Greek word that means sprinkle, occur in connection with baptism, anywhere in the New Testament?"

He replied: "I *candidly* answer that I do not know that it does. But you should not think that the quantity of water makes any difference. Baptism is the *application* of water, and just so that water is used, it is sufficient—a little answers as well as *much*."

"O, I see!" said Mellie, as a new idea flashed into her mind; "I see now the difference; you believe that the virtue or significance of baptism is in the water, or in the application of water, while I believe that it is in an action performed in water. You believe that the application of water is beneficial to the subject, while I believe that the action in water only illustrates or symbolizes a benefit already received. I now better understand the language of the Confession of Faith where it speaks of baptism being a 'sign and seal,' etc. I never before realized the difference that there appears to be in the objects intended by Baptists and Pedobaptists. They do not baptize for the same purpose, I discover. But to give you my reasons for believing the Baptists to be right, would require me to go back over the same ground that we have already traveled in this discussion, and as I do not expect to convert you to my belief, I will only give you one or two illustrations, which, I think, are to the point. When Pilate could not prevail on the people to release Christ, and they 'cried out, crucify Him,' he took water and washed his hands in the presence of the multitude, and said: 'I am innocent of the blood of this just man.' Pilate declared his innocence by words, and emblematically illustrated the fact by the washing of his hands in, or with water. The action spoke a language—it had a meaning—it was not to produce or insure his innocence, but to *declare* it. Again: To teach them a lesson of humility, Christ washed His disciples' feet. The illustration, the symbol, the emblematical import of the declaration was humility; but was this signified by the water? Most assuredly not, but by the act itself. Now, could this lesson of humility have been impressed by pouring or sprinkling a few drops of water on the disciples' feet? or on their shoes only? Would this act have illustrated innocence or humility? No. but it would have come just as near to it as the sprinkling of a few drops of water on a lady's false hair and ribbons, (as I saw the Methodist preacher do) represents a death to sin and a resurrection to a new life. The more I investigate the two theories, the more they seem to diverge from each other. I am amazed at the difference."

"But, Mellie," replied Dr. Farnsworth, "baptism by pouring represents the pouring out of the Holy Spirit, and the water is emblematical of the influence of, or the purification of the Spirit. Don't you see how this is?"

"Yes," said Mellie, "I comprehend *your idea* of it. It seems to me that you assume to do a thing that can't be done. The Spirit is poured out, *not in form*, but only in *power*. You cannot tell how the Holy Spirit works; therefore you cannot illustrate its manner of working. That the wind blows, we know; of its power we know; but *how* it blows we do not know, nor can we illustrate it. Can you, by pouring a few drops of water, illustrate the manner in which the sun pours his rays down on the earth on a hot summer day? No; because you can conceive neither the shape, form, nor manner of its action. Neither can you illustrate the manner of an act of the Holy Spirit. But immersion illustrates a *professed fact*, experimentally realized, an *effect* previously produced, and it beautifully illustrates some of the most important doctrines of the gospel. But I beg pardon, Doctor, for talking so long, and will close by suggesting that we read the Bible thoroughly, and pray for more light on the subject."

Dr. Farnsworth arose, saying: "I see that you are joined to your idols, Mellie, so I may as well let you alone; but I hope that *you*, sister Brown, will reconsider the matter, and become convinced of the impropriety of expressing sentiments that you know to be prejudicial to our church."

"I have taken but little part in the discussion to-day," said Mrs. Brown, "because I preferred to listen rather than talk, but I have noticed one thing, especially; that is, that you rely but little on the Bible to support the usages of our church; and if I should say some things not endorsed by you, if the Bible sustains me in it, I think that I would be justifiable. It seems to me that if you have to go to history to support a practice of the church that the Bible says not one word about, you should not be surprised if the people think very strange of you when you preach to them the duty of reading and obeying the Scriptures, and taking it as the man of their counsel. John Calvin was an honest man; he said that the original mode of baptism was immersion, but that the church had changed it to affusion. He received the Bible teachings on the subject, but thought that the church had the right to make the change. I don't believe that the church has any right to change one of Christ's ordinances. Then the great John Wesley, whose followers preach against immersion, said that it was 'the ancient manner of baptizing.' His writings are here in the library by the side of John Calvin's, and if you doubt what I say, you can get the books and read for yourself."

"I am much surprised, Sister Brown, said the Doctor, "to find your mind in such a state. I had become convinced that Mellie would go off from us, but I must express my deep sorrow that *you*, too, will persist in speaking against the doctrines and usages of our church, as you are doing. Your own self-respect should cause you to say less, or voluntarily leave the church."

Mrs. Brown replied: "To God and my own conscience I appeal for the rectitude of my purpose and conduct; and as God will judge me in the last day, I shall make His book the guide for my future course. I will not let the church dictate to me what I shall believe, or what I shall say."

The pastor left in not a very pleasant humor, reflecting on the weakness of the human intellect, especially when it has a leaning toward Baptist sentiments.

CHAPTER XIII.

THE CHURCH TRIAL—STRANGE VISITOR. ...

DOCTOR FARNSWORTH having, as he considered, used all the means in his power to influence Mrs. Brown to desist from her public criticisms regarding the usages of the church, summoned the Ruling Elders to a Session Meeting, and with expressions of regret for the necessity of such a course, laid before them the state of affairs in the Brown family. He thought himself not wanting in liberality of feeling, nor averse to a free exercise of opinions by others, and had no inclination to deny the right of conscience in all matters of religion. "But there are occasions," said he, "when 'forbearance ceases to be a virtue.' I have labored earnestly and faithfully with Sister Brown, but my efforts have been fruitless—my counsels to no purpose. She is immovably fixed—a firm and uncompromising Baptist. She disseminates doctrines, both publicly and privately, that are obnoxious to us, and detrimental to our cause. She does not withdraw from the church, and yet refuses to withhold a free expression of heretical opinions; thus she is guilty, not only of gross errors in doctrine, but of sowing discord in the church. We have patiently suffered this for many months, and, in my opinion, the time has now come when some action by the church is demanded. She must change her course, or, to speak without evasion, she must be excluded from our communion. Our self-respect requires that we do this, much as we may regret the necessity for it."

Elder Jeffreys was the first to speak, who said: "This erring member being a woman, we may as well let her enjoy her own opinions unmolested. She is not a preacher, and can do but little harm, I suppose. If we let her alone, she will, no doubt, soon settle down and become quiet again. It is woman's right to talk, and if Sister Brown enjoys it, let her have the gratification it affords her."

Elder Sprague objected to this policy. "Because" said he, "Mrs. Brown has already done our church much injury. She has the reputation of being a pious woman, which gives her a strong influence with the public. Her daughter, as well as herself, has been continually uttering sentiments detrimental to our church, and the leaven is spreading and affecting the whole community; and if it is not checked, it will work great harm in our church here. These two ladies—members, I might say, have already done us more harm than all the Baptists in the community. Members who don't endorse our doctrines and practice are a curse to us and for my part I favor their expulsion. Let us act boldly and promptly, and make short work of the case before us, as an example to others."

"Yes," said the pastor, "make an example of her, that others may fear—that is the plan. I know that Col. Brown and his family have been strong supporters to the church, but we can't permit one of our members to be continually inveighing against our doctrines and practice. The usage of our church will not sanction the retention of a member under such circumstances."

Elder Jeffreys raised his spectacles to his forehead, and with a knowing look at the pastor remarked: "Such cases of discipline have been very rare. Such members generally leave of their own accord, and, perhaps, a little longer forbearance in this case will relieve us of all trouble. And by what law will you try her? Where is the statute? What rule in our church government will apply to the case? Remember this is not a case of scandal; no crime is alleged against Sister Brown; she is charged with no offense against public morals, but she only entertains opinions that we think erroneous, yet not such as to impair her Christian character, or to create a suspicion as to her piety."

"It is true," remarked the pastor, "that our forms for the trial of such cases are not as explicit as I would desire, yet there are general principles laid down, covering this offense. On page 460 of the Confession of Faith, it is declared that 'an offense is anything in the principles of a church member which is contrary to the word of God; or which, if it be not in its own nature sinful, may tempt others to sin, or mar their spiritual edification.' Again, the rule is, that 'nothing, therefore, ought to be considered by any judicatory as an offense, or admitted as matter of accusation, which cannot be proved to be such from Scriptural or from the regulations and practices of the church, founded on Scripture.' The matter of accusation against Mrs. Brown, is clearly an offense against the 'regulations and practices of the church, founded on Scripture," therefore is, clearly within the meaning of the law, a subject of discipline. Heresy and schism are offenses to be dealt with according to our rules; and the apostle Paul, in his Epistle to the Romans, says: 'Mark them which cause divisions and offenses contrary to the doctrines you have learned; and avoid them.' In his letter to Titus, Paul says: 'A man that is a heretic, after the first and second admonition, reject; knowing that he that is such is subverted, and sinneth, being condemned of himself.' The usage of all the Christian churches is to exclude from their fellowship all members who openly avow sentiments opposed to their faith and practice. They could not be consistent and do otherwise."

"Yes," said Elder Sprague, "our Methodist brethren have a very plain, consistent rule on this subject in their Discipline, a copy of which I have with me. It is on page 144; edition published, 1859."

"Read it, Bro. Sprague," said the pastor.

Elder Sprague read as follows: "If a member of our church shall be clearly convicted of endeavoring to sow dissensions in any of our Societies, *by inveighing against either our doctrines or discipline*, such person so offending, shall be first reproved by the senior minister, or preacher of his circuit, and *if he persist in such pernicious practices*, he shall be expelled from the church."

.. "That's it," said the pastor, "that's the way to do it. We can't have a church platform wide enough to hold all the heterogeneous notions in the world. If those who do not agree with us, will not leave us, we must leave them."

Elder Jeffreys made a motion to adjourn, to meet at the residence of Col. Brown on a future day, but after some consultation and interchange of opinions, it was decided to send a committee to inform Mrs. Brown of the proceedings commenced against her, and to request her presence at the next meeting of the Session. The pastor instructed the committee to say to her, that if she would recant the alleged heresy, or *even agree to cease hereafter to speak against the doctrines and usages of the Presbyterian church*, all further proceedings would be stayed; but otherwise, she would force on them the necessity of excluding her from their communion.

The committee promptly called on Mrs. Brown, and very kindly tendered to her the forbearance of the church, provided she would promise not to speak against their faith and customs. They earnestly entreated her not to force on them the painful necessity of excluding her.

Mrs. Brown told the committee that she would not attend the meeting of the Session, and handed them the following written statements, which she wished to be understood as her final decision:"

"I have not acted hastily in forming my conclusions, nor am I now prepared to take any backward step. My wish, all my life, has been to be a Bible Christian; and with my conception of God's teachings, I cannot endorse the baptism of unconscious infants, nor believe that anything but immersion is Scriptural baptism, therefore can make no promise to abstain from a free expression of my opinions. I regret to be compelled to differ from those with whom I have so long and so pleasantly mingled in a church relation; and while I cherish the kindest feelings for the members generally, I cannot sacrifice the right of conscience. In a word, I will obey God rather than man."

The committee reported to the Session, "That,

"WHEREAS: Sister Amanda Brown has been charged with the offense of disseminating heretical opinions and *inveighing against our doctrines and customs.* and,

WHEREAS: She has been repeatedly admonished, and faithfully warned of the evil she was bringing on the church, and earnestly entreated to withhold her expressions of disapproval and still solemnly declares her intention to persist in her former course, we recommend her exclusion from the communion of the church."

With but few remarks, the report was adopted.

At the next regular meeting of the church, the pastor, in accordance with his duty as defined on pages 514 and 515, of the Confession of Faith, announced that certain charges of errors in doctrine, and habitual expressions, tending to produce discord in the church, had been made and sustained against Sister Amanda Brown and that the Session, after due deliberation, had, on behalf of the church, excluded her from their communion. He then read from the book (Confession of Faith): "When any offender has been adjudged to be cut off from the communion of the church, it is proper that the sentence be publicly pronounced against him." "The design of excommunication is to operate on the offender as a means of reclaiming him; to deliver the church from the scandal of his offense; and to inspire all with fear, by the example of his punishment."

He then pronounced the sentence in the following form:

"WHEREAS: Sister Amanda Brown hath been, by sufficient proof, convicted of publicly disseminating doctrines contrary to the faith and practice of the church, and after much admonition and prayer, obstinately refuseth to hear the church, and hath manifested no evidence of repentance, therefore, in the name, and by the authority of the Lord Jesus Christ, I pronounce her to be excluded from the communion of the church."

"It is due to Sister Brown, perhaps," he remarked," to say that there has been no impeachment of her moral character, no allegation against her piety. It was because of the dissemination of views opposed to our doctrine and practice as a church, that made her expulsion necessary. The harmony of feeling and unity of sentiment in a church, is of the highest importance to its welfare, and it became a matter of necessity to purge out the leaven of heresy that had begun to work. For as the Scripture doth truly say: 'How can two walk together except they be agreed?'"

The exclusion of Mrs. Brown from the church, as might well be supposed, was a subject of much talk in the community, and many were the guesses as to what would be her future course.

It was but a short time after the church trial until Mr. Jones, a neighbor, called on her, accompanied by a stranger, whom he introduced as Dr. Atwood, and who, she soon ascertained, was a preacher of that system of doctrines know as Campbellism. The title of Doctor, however, had relation to medicine, rather than to divinity.

Dr. Atwood had recently organized a small church in the town, and being desirous of gaining more members, and knowing Mrs. Brown to be a convert to immersion, he thought she would probably unite with his church. Several hours had been spent in conversation relative to the different denominational peculiarities, in which he had taken special pains to represent his own in the most favorable light. Finally his conversation was directed to Mellie, to whom he remarked: "I can see no reason why anyone who is inclined to be an immersionist, cannot unite with the Christians. There is a great similarity —in fact but little difference between them and the Baptists."

Mellie smiled, and softly and pleasantly inquired, "Are not all the believers in Jesus

Christ, Christians? The world has given the different denominations their names, and they accept them, and since the world has given you a name, too, why do you not accept it? Then, when you wish to be more explicit, say you are a Campbellite Christian, as distinguished from Baptist Christian, Methodist Christian, etc. And as regards a similarity between your doctrine and the Baptists, excepting the action of baptism, it appears to me, nothing can be farther from the fact. I understand you to believe that *baptism* is essential to salvation, while Baptists teach that *salvation* is essential to baptism. You deny the doctrine of inherent total depravity, which is the very foundation of Baptist theology. Baptists teach regeneration by the direct agency of the Holy Spirit, which you deny. Baptists teach that religion is spiritual in its nature, while you seem only to regard it as a mental exercise. You teach that regeneration is only a reformation of life, while Baptists believe that it is a radical change of the moral nature, followed by reformation as its fruits. You baptize to make disciples; Baptists baptize on a profession of discipleship. You are a stranger to me, but your doctrine is not new. I have read it from books; heard it from the pulpit; and find that you run in the familiar channel. It seems to me that your teaching is contradictory."

"Why, Miss," said the Doctor, "you interest me by your ingenuity, as much as you astonish me by your boldness. And now you will please point out some of the contradictions."

"Well," replied Mellie, "you profess to believe

that there was a necessity for the mediation of Christ, and that beside Him there is no Saviour, and yet you deny man's total depravity, or entire helpless condition. You deny the operation of the Holy Spirit only through the written word—deny the direct influence on the heart. It appears to me, that to make up a consistent system of theology, requires three things: 1st. Total ruin or moral depravity. 2nd. The mediation and atonement of Christ; and, 3rd. The application of the virtues of this atonement to the sinner's heart, so that its effects shall be experimentally realized. Taking out the idea of total depravity, you render useless the mediation of Christ; and in denying the experimental evidence of the work of the Holy Spirit in regeneration, you deny the efficacy of Christ as a sacrifice. Thus one part of your system overturns another, and, as a whole, it is inconsistent, contradictory and self-destructive. The world is beginning to realize this fact, although you may not be prepared at this time to admit it."

"Strange! Strange! Perhaps it is true that every generation gets wiser," said Dr. A.

After a few minutes spent by the Doctor in trying to extricate his doctrine from the charge of inconsistency, the following dialogue ensued:

Mellie.—You are a physician, are you not?

Dr. A.—I am.

Mellie.—You have administered medicine to the sick, I presume.

Dr. A.—I have.

Mellie.—Does your medicine usually have an

effect upon your patients?

Dr. A.—It does, generally.

Mellie.—When it has the desired effect, what is the result?

Dr. A.—When it has the desired effect, the disease is removed and the patient restored to health.

Mellie.—When the medicine has no effect, what is the result?

Dr. A.—In severe cases, the patient dies.

Mellie.—Well, Doctor, suppose there had been no such thing as disease, would you have undergone the labor and study of preparing yourself for the practice of medicine?

Dr. A.—Certainly not; because in that case a physician would be altogether useless.

Mellie.—Well, suppose that notwithstanding there is disease, that people need healing, and yet can experience no beneficial effects from the use of medicine - allowing that if medicine does the sick man any good, the fact is experimentally known—would there be any use for a physician?

Dr. A.—No; no more than in the other case.

Mellie.—Well, again: Suppose a malignant disease breaks out in the country, the people are all sick and in danger of death, but you, as a great philanthropist, prepare a remedy, and, through kindness, you proclaim that relief is in the reach of all, that the remedy is sure, and offered without money and without price—whosoever will, may apply and be healed. But if this be all that is done, will the people be cured?

Dr. A.—Of course not, unless the remedy is

applied—unless the medicine is taken according to the prescription.

Mellie.—When the medicine is taken, what must the effect be in order to prevent death?

Dr. A.—The disease must eradicated—the system cleansed, and the patient restored to health.

Mellie.—Could this be done and the patient not sensible of the fact—not know experimentally of the change or cure effected?

Dr. A.—I never knew a case in which the patient did not realize the change. If a sick man is made well, of course he knows it.

Mellie.—Well, Doctor, the Bible pronounces sin a disease, declares the whole human race to be affected by it, and in danger of eternal death. The virtue of the blood of Christ is offered as *the* remedy, to which all may come and be made whole. The Holy Spirit offers to apply this remedy to all who will come with faith in its merits. and promises that all who partake of it shall be made *new creatures*, and have God's Spirit to bear witness with theirs that they are passed from death unto life. Now, if the remedy is applied and the disease cured, the sinner must experimentally realize the effect—must experience a change of heart, of motives, of feelings, desires and aspirations. But if there were no disease, the remedy would be useless; unless applied, the remedy becomes of no avail, and if applied, and no effect produced, it is worthless, and if an effect is produced, and yet not sufficient to be sensibly ascertained by the sufferer, it is certainly of doubtful value."

Mellie was, in reality, a "Little Baptist" in theory, in every sense of the word. There seemed not to be a single doctrine or practice, common to the denomination, that she had not found a satisfactory reason for in the Bible. But, as will ever be the case with all who closely investigate it, the difference between the Baptists and all other denominations became more and more striking, the more she examined the subject. There are leading fundamental principles distinguishing them as a peculiar people, that cannot be given up without sacrifice of what they believe to be the vital doctrines of the gospel. and, taking TRUTH for their watchword, they will ever remain unmoved, though the rest of the Christian world stands arrayed against them. Having professed allegiance to Christ, they cannot shun to declare His truth as they understand it, nor depart from obedience to His laws.

CHAPTER XIV.

THE SATURDAY MEETING—FAMILY CONSULTATION.

IT was a beautiful Saturday morning in the month of May. Everything was astir at Colonel Brown's, getting ready to go to the Baptist meeting. Contrary to the expectations of Mrs. Brown and Mellie, Colonel Brown and Frank declined going with them. When the ladies arrived at the church, they found an unusually large congregation for a conference meeting. This church adhered to the old custom of holding a meeting once a month on Saturday, to attend to the general business of the church.

It has been said that "coming events cast their shadows before;" and at this time anticipations, that had ripened into a current report, had spread over the community, to the effect that Mrs. Brown and Mellie would join the church on that day, hence the large congregation. Many were there, prompted by mere curiosity, while some had gone in the capacity of spies, to take notes and report proceedings. The pastor preached a calm, dispassionate sermon, on "Christian Duty," which he discussed in three divisions: 1st. "Duty to God," 2nd. "Duty to the church," and 3rd. "Duty to the world." At the close of the sermon, the usual forms were observed, of inviting the church to sit in conference, and stating that the church was ready to receive applicants for membership. While the church engaged in singing that good old hymn: "Amazing grace, how sweet the sound," all eyes were turned in the direction of Mrs. Brown and Mellie, who sat with so much composure, that a general disappointment was visible all over the house. But while singing the fourth stanza, and after the words: His word my hope secures, Mellie arose alone, and with a calm, deliberate movement, evincing a fixed and steady purpose, took the designated seat. The pastor asked her to relate some evidences of her change of heart, which she proceeded to do in a voice so distinct, as to be plainly heard by the congregation. She said:

"I grew up, believing that nature and education had given me all the qualification for happiness that I needed, but by reading the Bible and becoming better informed, I found this to be untrue. My conscience bore testimony to the fact that I was a condemned sinner, meriting only the displeasure of God. I sought to gain His favor by good deeds, and by various means that all proved unavailing, until by long and bitter repentance, I was led to the cross of Christ. There prostrated in the depths of humility, pleading the merits of Him who died for me, and trusting and believing in Him, I found peace for my soul. I felt that I was accepted of Him, and my sins pardoned. I felt no longer burdened on account of sin, but happy in a Saviour's love. I feel today to thank God that He led me out of the delusions of sin, into this glorious light of his love. And though I have often since then felt a remorse of conscience for the neglect of duty, I have nevermore felt that sense of condemnation, as I once did. I feel that I love my Saviour, and I wish to follow Him, and in obedience to His command, be baptized, to be united with His people, and to serve Him while I live on earth."

No questions were asked, as all were satisfied; and she was, by a vote of the church, unanimously received as a proper subject for baptism after submitting to which, as the initiatory rite she would be entitled to all the privileges as a member of the church.

After returning home, Mrs. Brown informed her husband that it was Mellie's intention to be baptized the next day, and also told him that she had nearly made the decision to be baptized herself; that she felt it her duty to do so, and that her conscience could not be easy until she discharged this duty. To which Colonel Brown replied:

"I see no necessity nor reason for making this ado in the community, by changing your church relations in your old age. My family for several generations, have lived and died Presbyterians, and I trust that the most of them, at least, have gone to heaven. If *they* could go to heaven Presbyterians, why may not you, as well?"

"Well," said she, "I hope that all your relatives that are passed away, have gone to heaven, but what has that to do with my duty to my Saviour?

With me, it is not a question of going to heaven, but *only a question of duty.* I am not, as a Christian, a mere hireling, proposing to do certain things, for which I am to receive heaven as a reward. Salvation is a gift, but it is my duty to obey my Lord and Master."

"I know," said he, "that there is nothing to be gained by arguing the question with you, so do as you please. And as regards Mellie, you know that I have always said, 'her and her Bible for it.' I was anxious to see what would be a child's conclusion on the baptismal question, from reading the Bible free from all restraints, and prejudice. The problem is now about to be worked out, and I shall not object to her following her own judgment in the matter. She thinks that she is right, and she may do whatever she feels to be her duty. Whatever prejudice my education has given me, is against the Baptists, yet I am bound to admit that they are a very respectable denomination, and if what all history says of them is true, they are the most ancient denomination in existence. Except for the Roman Catholics, the Baptists are the most permanent religious organization in the world; because, resting their faith and practice alone on the Bible, and rejecting all creeds or systems of human invention, they are less liable to change than others, whose Conferences and Synods are authorized to legislate and change their rules and practices as policy may dictate. The Baptists have flourished in all countries when not under the ban of proscription, and here in America they bid fair to become the largest and most powerful denomination in the country.

"I have often thought that if precisely the same influences were brought to bear upon every person alike, there would not be half the difference in opinions that there is in religion. If all could be divested of the prejudices of education, there would be much more harmony in the interpretation of the Scriptures, and the great number of sects would be merged into one grand Scriptural Church. The different sects propagate the different notions, and thus the world is diverging from, rather than approaching harmony. But the Presbyterians are more respectable than the Baptists. Their preachers are more learned, and they hold higher rank in society, at least in this region."

Colonel Brown was a logical thinker, and well versed in the current history of the times; but he had a way of looking at every subject in the light of worldly interests, and worldly ambition. Rank in society was a grand idea with him. Every step was measured by the advantages to be gained by it. He courted popularity for himself, and was very jealous of every act of his family that might have a prejudicial influence. In this instance he saw that submission would be better than resistance, as to the effect on the public mind; so he acquiesced in his wife's decision, and promised to accompany her to the church on the next day, to appear, at least, that he made no serious opposition to the course his wife and daughter were taking.

Finding matters entirely beyond his control, Frank resolved to endure it all with as good grace as he possibly could, though he was far from approving the course of his mother and sister. Like his father he saw the wisdom of patiently enduring what he could not prevent, and ceased to cast any reflection upon them, further than was expressed by a very sad countenance. But there was another person in the family who took a very different view of matters; this was old Aunt Polly, the colored woman who had been a regular employee in the family as a house woman and cook. She came into the family room, saying:

"Bless de Lord! I's so glad de Missus and Miss Mellie is gwine to be Baptists. I'se been a Baptist thirty years, an' I know 'twill do; nobody's gwine to be dissatisfied wid der baptism after dat."

"Why is it, Aunt Polly," said Mrs. Brown, "that you colored people are nearly all Baptists?"

"Lor Missus," she replied, "nigger mity ignorant, but dey loves de truth. Den, you knows, dey have been raised to 'bey de commands of der Master, an' dey think of nothing else but to do as dey are told. So when dey becomes servants of Christ, all dey ask is what he have 'em do; and when dey see him go down into de river to be baptized, and den hear him say 'follow me,' dey go right along an' 'bey him, without trying to do some oder way, and den say dey didn't know no better."

That's right, Aunt Polly," said Mellie, "stick to the commandments and you will make no mistakes."

"Yes, bless you chile," said she, "I never know'd dat you were sich a strong Baptist before de day you talked wid dat Camerlite preacher. It done dis ole soul good to hear you; I des laft all over."

"Why, did you hear me talking to Dr. Atwood, Aunt Polly?" asked Mellie.

"Ah!" said she, "you're rite, I did. You see I finished cleanin' up de kitchen, and den I slip aroun' to hear what you all talkin' 'bout; an' when I hear you talkin' sich strong Baptist talk, I slip behind de door an' hear all you say. I'se so proud you such a true Baptist; but I jes 'spected dat, when, long time ago, I saw you readin' dat little Bible so much; an' many times dis ole soul prayed for dat, an' her prayers are now answered, thank the Lord."

"You don't seem to like the Campbellites much, I see," said Mellie.

"Whoopee! dis ole darkey'll never be no Camerlite. No, never. I knows too much 'bout 'sperimental religion for dat. People dat have larnin may talk about *doing* religion, an' working der way to heaven, but I can't see how dat is. I'se very ignorant, an' if I'se to 'pend on doing everything jes right, I might miss somethings an' den when I go to heaven dey not let me in. I wants dat good, old fashioned religion dat I can feel, for when I'se happy I knows it, an' feels I'se in de right road. It is little dat I knows about de readin' of de Bible, but der is one text dat I wouldn't give for all de Camerlite preachin' in de world. It's 'By grace are ye saved, through faith, and that not of yourselves; it is de gift of God: not of works, lest any man should boast.' Wise people may know some oder way to heaven, but dis ole soul is going to 'pend on Christ for de Saviour—she is now, shore Ah! when I hear a person say dat dare is no sich ting as a 'sperience of grace, it proves dat dey knows nothin, 'bout it, like demselves. Faith in de Lord, and grace in de soul; dat's de 'complishment for heaven—'tis now, shore."

Frank, who had been listening to these remarks, asked, "What is faith, Aunt Polly?"

"Lor, chile," said she, "dat's de easiest ting 'splained in de world. It is to take God at his word; to trust in his promises; to hold fast, an' never let 'em go. We don't try to do nothin' 'ceptin we have faith, but wid faith we can do all tings. Now don't you remember chile, when you was drivin' out in de carriage, an' comin' to de ole bridge on de creek, you were afraid to cross it. You thought maybe it was rotten, so you didn't have faith in it; an' you was gwine to hunt some oder way home, but a man happened to come along an' told you dat de bridge was sound an' safe, so you took his word for the truth; you have *faith*, you 'pend on de bridge, you drive on it, and come over safe an' sound. Now your faith caused you to go forward an get over de creek, an' dat's what I calls saving faith. Christ is able to save everybody, an if we have faith to venture on him, he will carry us safely over de stream of death, to de promised land. But if we have no faith in him an' try to find some oder way, he will not take us over no more dan de bridge did you while you would not venture on it for lack of faith. Long time ago I didn't have faith, den I sees heaps of troubles. I felt dat I was lost, an' didn't know how to find de way; but when I have faith, my troubles all gone, an' I feel glad. To have faith is to 'pend on de Saviour, to trust him, have confidence in him, an' venture on him an' never let him go."

"O, yes Aunt Polly," said Frank, "that all sounds very nice—it's quite an easy way, perhaps; but I thought that awhile ago you were going to be saved by obedience—by obeying the commands. Is not this your doctrine?"

"Lor, chile," said she, "whenever you have faith, an' 'pend on de Saviour, an' feel dat your sins are pardoned, den you gwine to love dat Saviour an' try to 'bey Him—dat's de gospel, chile. Den you'll want to be baptized, too, because He has commanded it. But people who go an' be baptized, an' 'bey de commands, all because dey 'fraid of going to hell, won't never get in heaven for dat—now dat's shore. Long ago, when 'us cullered' folks were in slavery, on ole Master's plantation, some of de niggers 'beyed orders an' (part of de time) worked first rate, just because dey were 'fraid of de lash; but dem were de meanest niggers on de plantation; you couldn't trust dem out of your sight. But some of 'em loved ole Master, an' delighted in 'beying orders an' working for him. Because dey loved him dey wanted to please him. Dem niggers would do to trust anywhere. An' dat's de way it is about serving de Lord. All dat jes 'beys commands 'cause dey 'fraid of hell, or to please de world or make 'emselves popular, don't love God—have no confidence in Him, and He has no confidence in dem. Dey are hypocrites—an' *dat's what's de matter.*"

Aunt Polly was conscientiously honest, and her deportment showed her to be a genuine Christian. One of the features distinguishing the ushering in of the Christian era, was "the poor have the gospel preached unto them;" and a highly commendable feature of that gospel, is, that it is plain and simple that the unlettered, as well as the learned, may comprehend its principles and realize its benefits. Of Christ it is said, "the common people heard Him gladly." While Aunt Polly could not read the Bible, enough of it had been taught to her for her to understand the principles of the gospel plan of salvation; and in relation of the experimental evidences of Christianity, she knew as much as the wisest; for Jesus said of His people, "they shall be all taught of God." She walked by faith, trusting to the internal evidences of the Spirit to assure her of her acceptance with God; and with a never flagging hope pointing her mind upward and a zeal for the Master's cause that never grew cold, she went humbly forward in the discharge of her duties, bearing daily testimony to the truth, that true religion has in it a power to control the conduct of its possessors. She was one of the few of her race that abhorred the wild fanaticism that so frequently characterizes their meetings, and adhered to a consistent life of faith and humility. She accepted her sphere in life; tried

CHAPTER XV.

—THE BAPTISM.

...the sun shone
...was
...tling
...ngly

...early
..., th...

...in
...his
...He
...ning
...d to
...the
...en
...all
...wild
...their
...life of
...phere in

to do her duty to both God and man; and had the confidence of all who knew her.

Those who choose one sect because of its aristocracy, and reject another because of the humble sphere of some of its adherents, may learn a lesson from this incident related by Mr. Spurgeon: An aristocratic professor of the religion of the humble Saviour, was on her death bed, and her pastor came to comfort her. As he talked to her of that glorious heaven in which she hoped soon to dwell, she interrupted him by saying: "My dear pastor, are there not two places in heaven? one for me, and one for Betsey in the kitchen? She is so unrefined!" The pertinent answer was: "You need not concern yourself, my sister, about the arrangements in heaven, for you will never get there unless you get clear of your cursed pride."

CHAPTER XV.

SUNDAY—THE SERMON—THE BAPTISM.

SUNDAY was a beautiful day; the sun shone with all its brightness; the sky overhead was serene and blue, and the green leaves, nestling in the breeze, made the day surprisingly delightful.

Col. Brown, with his entire family, were early at the church; and, at the appointed time, the pastor entered the stand, introducing the service by the usual preliminaries, and announced as a text "Blessed are they that do his commandments, that they may have a right to the Tree of Life, and may enter in through the gates into the city."—*Rev.* 22.4. He stated that the subject to be discussed, was: THE CHRISTIAN'S RIGHT TO THE TREE OF LIFE. "Man," said he, "was lost in the garden of Eden, as a consequence of his disobedience to the command of his Maker. He was driven from the garden, and a flaming sword, which turned every way, was placed to guard the way against man's approach to the Tree of Life. This was doubtless an evergreen tree, pointed out to man as an emblem of eternal life. The flaming sword in the hands of Justice, was an emblem of the wrath of God, because of man's transgression. God's law had been violated, His sovereign authority spurned; and Justice demanded satisfaction before man should again approach the Tree of Life and live forever. The decree of God had gone forth: 'Dust thou art, and unto dust thou shalt return.' 'The dust shalt return to the earth as it was, and the spirit to God who gave it.' Man must yield to this immutable decree and give up this mortal life and unassisted by Mercy, his spirit must return to God, only to be banished from His presence. But, 'God so loved the world that He gave His only begotten Son, that whosoever believeth in Him should not perish, but have everlasting life.' Christ fulfilled the law by a life of strict obedience to all of its moral requirements; offered Himself a sacrifice for man's transgression, and gave His own life as the price for man's redemption. Christ honored the law, and died in man's stead, that God might remain just, and man be saved. Possessing both a human and divine nature qualified Him for mediation between God and man. He suffered on the cross until Justice was satisfied, then, crying out, 'It is finished,' Justice and Mercy met together, and Righteousness and Peace kissed each other, before the altar of His sufferings. He died for our offenses, and was raised again for our justification. He has become the author of eternal salvation to all them that obey Him, and the end of the law for righteousness to every one that believeth.

"Yet, although Christ offered a meritorious sacrifice, and Justice demands no more, the flaming sword is not removed. It yet guards the way to the Tree of Life (through the law) as before. The law yet claims its penalties of all transgressors; it must have a perfect obedience, else none can gain access by its authority; but Christ, rendering this obedience and becoming the end of the law, has opened up through the gospel a new and living way. Christ said, 'I am the way;' and when the old prophet, Isaiah, had a vision of this way, it appeared to him so plain, that he said 'the wayfaring man, though a fool, need not err therein.' Yes, this way is plain. 'Believe on the Lord Jesus Christ and thou shalt be saved.' Faith leads to love and obedience. 'Ye are my friends if ye do whatsoever I command you.' This way is said to be narrow, yet it is plain and clear of obstructions. It is so easy of access that whosoever is willing to walk therein may readily find it. But it must be entered through the strait gate of selfdenial. This is only difficult because just on the other hand, the broad road, that leads to destruction, is entered by the wide gate of self-indulgence.

"Would you walk in this new way that has been opened to the Tree of Life, and escape the edge of the flaming sword? Then enter in with humility and prayer; enter it with repentance and faith, and such faith as produces love and willing obedience to all the commands of Christ. When He came out of the baptismal waters of the Jordan, the Holy Spirit, in the likeness of a dove, came down to attest that He is the Son of God, and after His conference with Moses and Elias, on the mount of Transfiguration had ended, a voice from the cloud was heard saying: 'This is my beloved Son; hear ye him.' Those who hear and obey the Son of God, shall have a right to the Tree of Life, and may enter in through the gates into the city. The Christian will enter Heaven by a right derived from Jesus Christ. His followers have a title to Heaven that is sealed with the blood of the everlasting covenant; and as an earnest of their inheritance, they have the Holy Spirit to bear witness that their rights are secure.'

The sermon of which this is but a brief outline, was closed with a glowing description of the holy city, the new Jerusalem, which the lovers of Jesus shall one day enjoy. The effect on the congregation was almost magical. All were electrified by the eloquence of the speaker; and the subject had taken hold on the minds of very many present. There was many a "weeping Mary," and "trembling jailer," ready to inquire, "What must I do to be saved?" and not a few of the old hardened sinners were made to feel their need of salvation, and with Agrippa of old, to say, "Almost thou persuadest me to be a Christian." The full results of the Sermon will be known only in eternity.

The pastor then requested all who desired to witness the administration of baptism, to repair to the ford of the little river, but a short walk from the church. "This," said he, "might have been as well attended to here at the church. We have a baptistery that affords water sufficient for the purpose, but the young lady to be baptized prefers going to the river, as it more resembles the earliest customs of the disciples. It is some more trouble, to be sure; but a little inconvenience should never be weighed in the scale against duty. I am, myself, partial to baptizing in a river, or a place of much water, because it seems more fully to follow in the footsteps of my Master, who, in my imagination, I can see going down the banks of the river Jordan, where His forerunner, John the Baptist, laid Him beneath the yielding wave, and raised Him up again, thereby prefiguring His death and resurrection." Arriving at the water, the pastor took an eligible position, and announced that the church was present and ready to hear the profession of faith of any other person who might feel disposed to confess Christ before the world, by being baptized in His name, and after His example. That it was the duty of all Christians to obey the commands of Christ, and that baptism is the first duty enjoined after believing and realizing pardon.

Mrs. Brown went forward; told something of her experience from the time of her conviction of sin, until she found peace by trusting in Christ. She referred to the trials she had encountered on her Christian journey, and especially of her change of views relative to baptism, which had led her to pursue the course that she was then taking. What she had received for baptism had failed to bring the answer of a good conscience toward God, and she wished to be baptized after the example given by Christ.

All knew her to be an exemplary Christian, and the church was unanimous in her reception.

Mr. Coleman was not a controversialist;

whatever he believed he preached as *truth*, and not a debatable question. He would give his own views in plain terms, but seldom alluded to the views of others, or even intimated that others differed from him. His motto was: "Preach the truth, and error will give way before it."

"Here are two sisters," said he, "who have come forward to receive baptism at the hands of this church. This is the way that a public profession of discipleship of Christ is made. They are here to submit to the initiatory rite of a Christian church—to take the oath of allegiance to the King of kings and Lord of lords. Baptism does not originate the obligation to serve Christ, but it is a public acknowledgment of it. It must be a voluntary, personal act, else it fails to be obedience. It does not actually wash away sin, but is emblematical of it. It is a symbolical illustration of death and the resurrection. The body is buried beneath the waves, emblematical of dying and going from sight; it is raised again, typifying the resurrection from the dead. As a declarative action, baptism signifies a death to sin and a resurrection to a new life; it also declares the believer's faith in a once dead, but risen Saviour. It declares our faith, that though our bodies must die and be buried or hid from sight, they shall yet, by the power of God, come forth again in the Saviour's likeness. Baptism is an ordinance of the New Testament; it belongs exclusively to the Christian gospel dispensation. The authority for it is Christ himself. The obligation to perform it is just as binding on believers as any other command of the gospel. Would we be faithful to our Master, we must neglect none of His commandments. Here are two persons that have had water poured or sprinkled on them, but this has failed to satisfy their consciences, because that was not the action that Christ commanded nor the example that He gave. They now propose to be buried with Him by baptism. After this, they will doubt no more that they have been Scripturally baptized. None doubt this; all denominations of Christians accept immersion as Scriptural baptism. Then, is it not best to accept that which no one doubts, instead of that which so many dispute, and with which so many become dissatisfied? Were I to offer any of you choice of two bills of money, telling you at the same time that everybody endorsed one as a genuine bill but that there was a dispute about the other—that by many it was suspected of being a counterfeit, which would you take, the one doubted, or the one that was good beyond question? Sprinkling and pouring are by many doubted, and with them, many become dissatisfied; but that immersion is genuine baptism, is undisputed and *indisputable*. It is Scriptural; it satisfies the conscience; and illustrates the most important doctrines of the gospel."

After singing a hymn and offering a prayer to the Throne of Grace for guidance to the persons about to profess the Savoir before the world by an ordinance of Christ's appointment, the pastor led the ladies down into the limpid stream, and in the presence of a large assembly of spectators, the mother and daughter were laid beneath the yielding wave—illustrating a death to sin; and raised again—illustrating the rising to a new life.

Coming up out of the water, Mrs. Brown remarked: "Now I have a conscience void of offense toward God, that I could not have while living in disobedience to His command."

She exhorted others to go and do likewise.

Mellie's face wore a smile of surpassing sweetness. Calm and deliberate in her manner, she repeated the language of the text, "Blessed are they that do His commandments." Then she said: "Thank God for the Bible; it has taught me how to love the Saviour, and how to obey Him."

Col. Brown and Frank were deeply affected by the services of the day; and hopes were inspired that soon there might be another baptized household after the apostolic pattern.

A few days afterward, Col. Brown told his wife that Mr. Coleman's sermon had knocked the scales from his eyes in reference to the importance of trusting in Christ for salvation; that he had never before understood why he could not be saved by simply being a moral, honest and upright man. He had never thought of the fact that the flaming sword had not been taken down, but still turned every way to guard the way to the Tree of Life. This view of the subject alarmed him, and he saw that the only way to be saved was by trusting in Christ, who is the way, the truth, and the life. Like thousands of others, Col. Brown had never realized the distinction between the law and the gospel, but when he saw the necessity of a perfect obedience to the law, in order to escape the sword of Justice, he was enabled to comprehend the advantages offered to man in the gospel, by securing an entrance through the new and living way that Christ has opened for the salvation of His followers.

Reader, you cannot be saved by a law-righteousness, because the sword still guards the way to the Tree of Life—it has never been taken down. If thou art unconverted, get into that strait and narrow way that Christ has prepared. Strive to enter in at the strait gate, for many will seek (otherwise) to enter, and shall not be able. All who obtain a passport from Christ, will have an undisputed right to enter in through the gates into the Holy City, and to pluck the golden fruits from the Tree of Life, and live forever. Think not of a law-righteousness. "By the deeds of the law no flesh can be justified; but Christ is the end of the law for righteousness unto every one that believeth."

> "The law condemns, and makes us know
> What duties to our God we owe;
> But 'tis the gospel must reveal
> Where lies our strength to do His will."

CHAPTER XVL.

COMMUNION.

"MELLIE," said Nannie Gordon "there is one thing that will always keep me from being a Baptist. I believe in immersion, but I can't approve of your close communion. Why, last Sunday when Dr. Farnsworth invited all Christians of every name to come to the Lord's Table, there sat you and your mother, and a number of other Baptists, all looking on, and not one of you accepted the invitation. I can't see how you can do so. Does your mother think that because she has joined the Baptists, she is too good to commune with Presbyterians any more!"

"Now, Nannie" said Mellie, "wouldn't it have looked strange for her to have gone and communed with them? Had they not just excluded her from their church? and for nothing else only because she said that nothing but immersion was Scriptural baptism, and that infants ought not to be baptized at all? Do you suppose they wanted her to commune with them?"

"O, yes, Mellie; she is now a member of another church, and we invite all members in good standing in other churches, to come to our communion," said Nannie.

"But, Nannie, do you think that being a member in another church, makes my mother any better than she was when they excluded her from their communion? She has joined a church holding the very same doctrines for which she was excluded from the Presbyterians, and now, where is the consistency in inviting her, or any other Baptist, to their communion? Why should any church invite to the communion, members of other churches holding doctrines for which they would exclude one of their own members? The Baptists, Nannie, are consistent. They would exclude a member for teaching or practicing infant baptism; or for sprinkling and pouring for baptism, and they will not commune with the members of any church that believes and practices these things. Do you see any consistency in a church excluding a member one day, and the next day inviting that excluded member to commune with them, without asking any confession? If this is consistency, it is strange consistency."

"Well," said Nannie, "I don't know anything about it. I always thought the Baptists wrong about communion; perhaps it's only because I have heard others say so. I never took the trouble to look into the cause myself. It may be, after all, that they have a good reason for their course."

"You know very well," said Mellie, "that all my partiality for the Baptist church has been derived from the Bible; it was not so from choice, but because my understanding of the Scriptures compelled me to it. My early teachings were opposed to everything in that direction, but since I came to read and understand for myself, I can only wonder that all Christians are not Baptists. I can't see how they can take the Bible for a guide and be anything else.

"Now, Mellie tell me candidly, don't you think that all Christians ought to commune together?" asked Nannie, with much earnestness as though she had the whole argument in a nutshell.

"*Certainly I do*," replied Mellie, "but the very argument that proves that they ought to commune together, proves that they ought to live together in the same church. They ought all to do just what the Bible tells them to do, and if they did they could all live together and commune together, too. But how can we have harmony without agreement, or communion with out union? We do not want a mere pretended union when no real union exists. While each denomination has opposing doctrines and practices from every other, I can see no better way than for each to attend to its own business in its own way, and let the others do the same."

"I think they do that near enough," said Nannie.

"Yes," said Mellie, "they do in everything except communion. Other denominations never invite the Baptists to take a part in their church matters only when it comes to communion, and then it sometimes looks like they do it just to get an excuse to abuse us for not participating; and if they thought we would, perhaps they would not give us such pressing invitations. But then you know, Nannie, that the denominations are generally agreed that none but baptized persons have a right to partake of the Lord's Supper. And they agree, too, that immersion is Scriptural baptism. Therefore, on this ground, others can, without a sacrifice of principle, invite the Baptists. But while the Baptists deny that anything else than immersion is baptism, they can't invite others without sacrifice of principle that would bring them into confusion. Don't you see that upon this common ground, the Baptists must remain close communionists, or else endorse sprinkling and pouring as valid baptism?"

"Well, but Mellie, your church don't invite every one that has been baptized by your own ministers. There is Mr. Halladay, who once belonged to your church, you know, but since he quit and joined the Methodists *to be with his wife*, he is not invited to the Baptist communion, any more than if he had been only sprinkled by the Methodists. And you can't say that he has not been baptized, for Mr. Coleman, your own pastor, baptized him."

"Yes, yes," said Mollie; "I am glad that you mentioned that case, for it brings out the question on its merits. There is the point that other denominations can't see, or, rather, as it seems, *won't see*. It is not baptism *alone* that gives the right to a seat at the Lord's Table; if it were, every baptized reprobate that had ever been excluded from the church, might claim it. It is, strictly speaking, membership in the church that gives the right. Baptism only gives a *conditional* right. No one can be a member in a Baptist church without baptism, and none can come to the

Lord's Table without membership. So you see there are two conditions to be considered, instead of one. Baptists hold that repentance and faith are prerequisite to baptism, and that baptism is a prerequisite to membership, and that all these are prerequisite to communion. Baptists do not assume the authority of legislating for the Lord. They regard Christ as their Head and Lawgiver, and the church His executive, to see that His laws are properly enforced. They regard the communion table as the Lord's, and not theirs; and they, therefore, feel authorized to only admit those who have the legal qualifications."

"Well," said Nannie, "I declare I never thought you had such arguments as these in your favor. I have always heard it charged that it was just a kind of bigoted inconsistency in the Baptists that made them so restricted in communing, but you seem to offer a *reason* for all you do."

"0 yes," replied Mellie, "but you begin to see that the bigotry and inconsistency are on the other side, if any there be. It is strange that they should manifest such earnest desire to commune with us, when, if we were members with them, holding and teaching as we do, they would exclude us as they did my mother."

"Come, Mellie, don't charge us with more than we are guilty of. I hope we are not so inconsistent as that," said Nannie.

"Why, Nannie, have not the Presbyterians refused to let my mother live in the church with them? And, then, have they not afterward invited her to commune with them, and some of them even abused her for not doing so? Now, the Baptists will not commune with any that they will not live with, nor will they live with those that they will not commune with, and, again, they will not commune with those who will not live in the church with them. And this I call true consistency," said Mellie.

As Nannie stood reflecting and seemed to have nothing more to say, Mellie continued:

"I investigated all these things before I joined the Baptist church, and I fully understand and approve of them. I think that we are much nearer right, and a great deal more consistent, than those who abuse us for our convictions of duty, and then invite us to commune with them, contrary to our known wishes. Now, there is Mr. Smith, the Methodist preacher, who always invites the members of all denominations to participate in the Lord's Supper, but if you have noticed him closely, you have seen that he almost invariably says some hard things about the Baptists, as though he wished to hurt their feelings, so as to be sure to keep them back. And, then, too, he said in a sermon that the doctrine of Predestination and Election, as taught by the Presbyterians, 'had its origin with the Devil,' and that to it 'thousands would owe their damnation in hell.' He is a very rough spoken man, you know, and Dr. Farnsworth felt his cuts so sensibly that he said 'the people ought not to go to hear such a man preach.' Still they invite each other to the Lord's Table, and partake of the elements together, just as though there was a perfect agreement between them. Mamma says that she thinks open communion, so-called, is a *hobby* to delude the people, and keep up a prejudice against the Baptists. Any one can see that there is no consistency in abusing and accusing each other of teaching false doctrines, and then coming together to celebrate the Lord's Supper. By this they say to the world, 'Behold, how good and how pleasant it is for brethren to dwell together in unity,' and yet there is no unity, nor do they dwell together. They publicly profess what does not exist. As they profess in communion that they dwell together in unity, why don't they bury their differences and all unite in one church organization? Baptists say, one Lord, one faith, and one baptism—hence, one church, or order of churches, and, then, one communion table. Those who will not agree with them in this, they leave to their own choice. They strive to obey the laws of Christ as they understand them, and ask nothing of their opposers but to be left to follow their honest convictions of duty."

"Well, indeed," said Nannie, "I confess that you have greatly enlightened me on this subject. I never before saw the standpoint from which the Baptists look at the communion question; and I find that looking from different standpoints very materially changes the appearance of things. I must agree that the practice of the Baptists is entirely consistent with their faith in the premises. I never thought about membership and fellowship in the church, nor about unity of faith having anything to do with it, nor that open communion churches commune with those whom they will not live in the church with, and who, if permitted, would not live with them. This is such a ridiculous absurdity, that I don't see why they have not abandoned it long ago. I, for one, will never again speak harshly of the Baptists for their restricted communion."

"I am right glad to hear you say so, Nannie," said Mellie, "and I wish that all others could arrive at the same conclusion. It would greatly advance the cause of religion if all attended strictly their own business and let others alone. You girls in school, a long time ago nicknamed me, you know; I did not like it then, but now I am proud of the honor of being called 'THE LITTLE BAPTIST.'"

"I *do wish* that all could agree and go along together, it would be *so much better*," said Nannie.

"*I* do with all my heart," replied Mellie. "Christ prayed that all His people might be ONE; and if they were only united, they would form a mighty host, before which infidelity and all the powers of evil would be bound to give way, and the knowledge of the Lord would soon cover the earth. It is the dissensions among Christians, begetting jealousies and envyings, that fosters the spirit of infidelity, and retards the conversion of the world. If all would unite upon the teachings of Christ and the apostles, the Baptists would stand in harmony with them, and strife would be at an end. Baptists are not to blame for the multiplicity of sects, for they believe all that the Scriptures teach, and are willing to practice it.

Others believe all that Baptists do, and if they would only stop there, we could all easily unite, but they will go beyond what is revealed in the Bible, and teach 'for doctrines the commandments of men.' Then, because we will not follow them in these traditions they turn upon us with the cry of 'bigotry,' 'selfishness' and 'close communion.' For instance, the Scriptures teach that believers in Christ are proper subjects for baptism; Baptists say this, and other Christians agree with them. No one questions this position; it is undisputed ground. But, then, others persist in teaching that unconscious infants are also proper subjects for baptism, and as Baptists cannot find authority for it in the Bible, they cannot agree to it. Again, all Christian denominations agree with the Baptists that immersion is Scriptural or valid baptism. At least, they accept the immersed as Scripturally baptized; and if they would only practice what all, in common, agree is right upon this point, there would be an end of controversy. But they go beyond this and practice forms that have neither example nor precedent in the Bible; hence Baptists object to them as infringements on the laws of Christ, and do not adopt them. If all would consent to only practice that for which a plain precept or example can be shown in the New Testament, then, as a band of soldiers in one common cause, we might go forward under the Saviour's banner, to conquest and victory."

"I am afraid," said Nannie, "that you attach too much importance to baptism. If it does not wash away sin, but consists only in the use of water as a ceremony, what difference can it make whether there is much or little water used?"

"The difference, Nannie," said Mellie, "is that Christ told us what to do, and went himself down into the river Jordan, and gave us the example. Another very striking difference is in the design of the ordinance. Baptists use water, or perform the action in water, with an entirely different design from all others. Somebody is wrong—somebody is unscripturally baptized; first, in the mode or action, and secondly, in the design. A wrong design must destroy the validity of the ordinance, as well as a wrong mode. Therefore, if the Baptists are right as to design and mode, all others are wrong; but if others are right as to design and mode, then the Baptists are wrong, and hence, unscripturally baptized."

"You will confer a favor by enlightening me relative to the difference in design," said Nannie.

"Well, if you will patiently hear me," said Mellie, "I will try to do so. Without confining certain Pedobaptist denominations to their written creeds, but allowing that they have outgrown them, we will suppose that all agree that baptism is not a saving ordinance, but only declarative in its significancy. With the Disciples, unless designed as a saving ordinance, it means simply nothing, except as an illustration of death and the resurrection. As regards the person baptized, it declares nothing, past, present nor future. Though Scriptural in action, it is incomplete in design. Pedobaptists are confined to no specific mode or action, therefore, it must be the water alone that declares the design. Some say that by the pouring of water, they illustrate the pouring out of the Holy Spirit on the heart. Others assume that the water represents the purifying influence of the Spirit; while others, still, say it is merely a dedicatory ceremony, employing the use of water, at the hands of a Priest or Minister, and that its virtue, efficacy, significancy, or whatever it may be called, is derived from the official position of the Priest or Minister applying it. But it is clear that the pouring out of the Holy Spirit is not in form, but only in power, and this action can no more be represented by the pouring of water, than could the pouring down of the heat of the sun on a hot summer day. Water, in itself, does not represent or illustrate purification, for this is only done by washing—immersing or submerging. Purification or cleansing comes by the *act* of washing the thing *in* or *with* water, and not by pouring or sprinkling water on the object to be cleansed. Nor can we believe that the hands of the Priest, his official position, or his prayers, add any holy influence to the water; to do so would be to admit baptismal regeneration at once.

"Baptism consists of an action in water, or of a performance declaring the subject's death to sin, and resurrection to a new life. To show that it is *the action* and not the water, that represents and declares a thing or fact, let me give you some examples by way of illustration. Pilate declared his innocence of the blood of Christ by the simple act of washing his hands in the presence of the people. It was not the water but the act of washing in the water, that declared his innocence. Christ washed his disciples' feet as a declaration of humility. Humility was here expressed; but how? Did the water, or the application of water express it? Could sprinkling or pouring water have done it? No, none of these; but the act of washing the feet expressed it in a beautiful and striking figure. Baptism, in one place, is referred to as 'the washing of regeneration,' and again, as a ceremony symbolizing purification. But what is it that gives it this signification? It is simply because things are cleansed or purified by being washed in water, and the submerging—immersion—washing of a person in water, figuratively declares a spiritual cleansing or purification. But *the figure is always in the action, never in the water.* As Pilate declared his innocence by washing his hands, and Christ exhibited his humility by washing his disciples' feet, so in immersion we declare a death to sin and a rising again to a new life. Immersion declares the washing of regeneration, the cleansing from sin, and expresses faith in a once dead but risen Saviour. Coming up from the watery grave, we profess a renewal of heart, and exhibit a purpose to walk in newness of life. Like the children of Israel, who, by the passage through the Red Sea, renounced the land of Egypt, and confirmed their allegiance to Moses as their deliverer, and exhibited their confidence in him as their leader we, in baptism, renounce the dominion of sin, pledge allegiance to Christ, and take upon us an obligation to follow him as our leader. The parallel is so striking, that the apostle could justly say that the children of Israel were 'all baptized unto Moses in the cloud and in the sea.' In the days of Moses this would have been an unmeaning expression, because baptism, as a religious illustrative ceremony, was then unknown. But when known, and its teachings understood, as in the days of the apostles, the two afforded a beautiful analogy.

"Christ instituted in his church two ordinances: Baptism and the Lord's Supper. These two, figuratively illustrate all the important doctrines of the gospel. Baptism is emblematical of Christ's death and resurrection; declares a death to sin, and a purpose to lead a new life, and typifies the death and resurrection of our bodies; while the bread and wine used in the celebration of the Supper are emblems representing Christ's broken body and shed blood, by the use of which we declare our faith in his second coming. The participation in this is not to show our love for family and kin, our respect for our friends, nor confidence in the christianity of our neighbors. It was instituted in the church, and should be observed by the church only in a church capacity. The right of a church to administer communion, extends no further than her right to exercise discipline. Those who are not under her discipline cannot claim her most sacred privilege. The purpose is remembrance of Christ crucified for us, and as oft as the church exhibits these emblems, she shows forth the Lord's death, and declares to the world that Christ will come again. Baptism is a prerequisite to membership in the church, which must be legally and Scripturally obtained prior to the granting of the right to a seat at the Lord's Table."

"Then, you presume to say that there is but one church, I suppose," said Nannie.

"I presume to say," said Mellie, "just what you and all others must admit is true: that is, *there is not, and cannot be, but one Scriptural church*. I say nothing against the piety and religious deportment of the many Christian denominations, or churches, if you prefer the term; but for a church to be *Scriptural*, it must conform its doctrine and practice to the Scriptures If you grant that any one denomination is strictly Scriptural in its faith, practice and organization, you can but admit that all others are unscriptural in proportion as they differ from this one. No two that differ can be equally Scriptural. Two opposites cannot be alike, or in the same place."

"I understand you, now," said Nannie, "and begin to see that you Baptists are not so illiberal, after all, as you are usually charged of being. You mean that errors in the doctrine and practice of a church, do not necessarily destroy its claim to christianity, but only invalidates its claim to be a Scriptural organization; that while a wrong design and a wrong action in baptism may destroy its claim to be a Scriptural church, this does not unchristianize the membership, nor render them unworthy of confidence and respect as Christian people. It is not about whether we are *Christian* churches or not, that the Baptists raise the question, but as to whether we are *Scriptural* churches. Well, that's not so bad. If we are strictly Scriptural in our practice and organizations, the Baptists are not, as a matter of course. And, I suppose if they are right we are not; because it is impossible for all denominations to be exactly right and yet differ as they do. To be Scriptural is to be right, and to be contrary to Scripture is to be wrong. Therefore, somebody is wrong, because there is a disagreement. If the Baptists immerse, and the Pedobaptists sprinkle and pour for baptism, one or the other is wrong, sure. Now, both might be wrong, that is possible; but for both to be right, is *impossible.* Then, if the *design* as to the thing signified in baptism, is different, one or the other is mistaken; and if the design of the one is Scriptural, that of the other is unscriptural—this is plain. I think this question ought to be settled before there is any more *fuss* about close communion. But tell me Mellie, how do you get up so many ideas, with some text of Scripture always ready to apply as proof?"

"The main reason," replied Mellie, "is that I always *think,* as well as read."

AN ADDRESS TO THE READER.

WE now leave our little heroine to a life of duty, that is just opening up before her. The general lot of mankind must be her's—a life of trials, temptations, labors and duties. But she is armed for the conflict, for "she has chosen that good part, which shall not be taken from her." She has given her heart, and submitted her will to God, in whom she trusts for direction and support. She is a Christian, not for popularity or convenience, but from principle. She is not a Christian by profession only, *but a Christian in fact*. The Bible is made her guide in all matters of duty. By her, it is accepted as a revelation from heaven, and adopted as the rule of her faith and practice. And whether her life be spent in the quiet home, in the more public activities, or in teaching the way of life and salvation in lands of heathen idolatry, she has an assurance that the God whom she serves will never forsake her. She has enlisted in the army of the Lord with a firm and steady purpose that insures fidelity to his cause; and whether she lives to a good old age, or is early called to her reward, we leave her with an assurance that her end will be peace.

How many of the readers of this little book will strive to follow the example of little Mellie Brown, by reading the Bible to learn what it teaches, and obeying its commands? Perhaps there is not but one that is ready to answer: "I want to understand the Bible, and to do whatever is right." Then begin to learn while you are young. You have seen how easy it is for a child, who reads without prejudice, to understand the plain commands of Christ. Also, how hard it was for Mrs. Brown to give up her prejudices, and embrace the truths that were so easy for Mellie to receive. You have seen, too, that as good as everybody called little Mellie Brown in her childhood, and as good as she really thought herself to be, she yet needed a new heart to qualify her for the church and for heaven. You have also observed that Colonel Brown, in his old age, just awoke to the truth that he had all his life been deluded with the thought that he would be saved by his morality and honesty. He discovered at last, that his faith had been resting on a false foundation, and must be directed to Christ for salvation. We left Frank Brown, who had been baptized in his infancy, and had grown up *nominally* in the church, a moral, but haughty, independent and self-willed young man, serving the god of worldly popularity. I trust that he, and all such characters, may early see and feel the necessity of being born again as a preparation for the kingdom of heaven. The Lord has said, "Son, give me thy heart," and has promised, "they that seek me early shall find me." The dying advice of the Psalmist David to his son, was, "Solomon, my son, know thou the God of thy fathers; serve him with a perfect heart, and with a willing mind, for the Lord searches all hearts, and understandeth all the imaginations of the thoughts. If thou seek him early, he will be found of thee, but if thou forsake him, he will cast thee off forever."

"Destruction's dangerous road,
  What multitudes pursue;
While that which leads the soul to God,
  Is sought and known by few.

Believers enter in,
  By Christ, the living gate;
But those who will not leave their sin,
  Complain it is too strait.

If self must be denied,
  And sin forsaken quite:
They rather choose the way that's wide,
  And strive to think it right.

Encompassed by a throng,
  On numbers they depend—
So many surely can't be wrong,
  And miss a happy end.

But numbers are no mark,
  That men will right be found:
A few were saved in Noah's Ark
  For many millions drowned.

Obey the gospel call,
  And enter while you may:
The flock of Christ is always small,
  And none are safe but they.

Lord, open sinners' eyes,
  Their awful state to see,
And cause them 'ere the storm arise,
  To thee for help to flee."

APPENDIX

The following compend is copied from the "Baptist Outlook," published under the editorial management of E. T. Hiscox, D.D., New York. It speaks for itself, therefore, is inserted here without comments:

BAPTIST WAYMARKS.
BAPTISM.

MEANING OF THE WORD.

The term *baptize* is, originally and properly speaking, a Greek word. Rightly to understand its meaning, we should seek the opinions of those skilled in the Greek language. Men who are familiar with its terms ought to know. How do the dictionaries define it? What do the lexicographers and scholars say?

DONNEGAN says it means "To *immerse* repeatedly into liquid, to submerge, to soak thoroughly, to saturate."

SCHLEUSNER says: "Properly, it signifies to *dip*, to immerse, to immerse in water."

SCAPULA says: "To *dip*, to immerse, as we do any thing for the purpose of dyeing it."

PARKHUBST says: "To *dip*, immerse or plunge in water."

ALSTIDIUS says: "To baptize signifies *only* to *immerse*, not to wash, except by consequence."

SCHREVELLIUS says: "To baptize, to merge, to bathe."

GREENFIELD says: "TO *immerse*, immerge, submerge, sink."

PASSON says: "To *immerse* often and repeatedly, to submerge."

SCHOETTGEN says: "To merge, *immerse*, to wash to bathe."

STEVENS says: "To merge, or *immerse*, to submerge or bury in the water."

STOURDZA says: "Literally and always it means to *plunge*. Baptism and immersion, therefore, are identical."

STEPHANUS says: "To *plunge* under, or overwhelm in water."

STOCKIUS says: "Properly, it means to *dip*, or immerse in water."

LIDDELL AND SCOTT say: "To *dip* repeatedly."

ROBINSON says: "To *immerse*, to sink."

ANTHON says: "The primary meaning of this word is to *dip*, to immerse."

GREEN says: "To *dip*, immerse, to cleanse or purify by washing."

MOSES STUART says: "Baptizo means to *dip*, plunge, or immerse into any liquid. All lexicographers and critics of any note are agreed in this."[a]

ROSENMULLER says: "To baptize is to *immerse* or dip the body, or part of the body which is to be baptized, going under the water."[b]

TURRETIN says: "The word baptism is of Greek origin which signifies to baptize, to dip into, to *immerse*."[c]

WILSON says: "To baptize, to *dip* one into water, to plunge one into the water."[d]

LEIGH says: "The nature and proper signification of it is to *dip* into water, or to plunge under water."[e]

VOSSIUS says: "To baptize signifies to plunge."[f]

WETSTEIN says: "To baptize is to plunge, to *dip*.

The body, or part of the body, being under water is said to be baptized." *g*

CAMPBELL says: "The word *baptizein*, both in sacred authors and in classical, signifies to dip, to plunge, to *immerse*, and was rendered by Tertullian, the oldest of the Latin Fathers, *tingere*, the term used for dyeing cloth, which was by immersion." *h*

To the same effect is the testimony of many other scholars and critics familiar with the Greek language. Candid minds, after a suitable examination, can have little question that the true meaning—indeed, the only proper meaning—of baptizo is to dip, plunge, immerse, or bury in water, and that baptism can only be performed by such an act.

SIGNIFICANT USE OF BAPTIZO.

Why did our Saviour and His apostles make use of this particular word *baptizo* to express or describe the ordinance which He committed to His churches and enjoined on all His disciples? The Greek language is rich in terms to express all positive ideas, as well as varying shades of meaning. Why was this one word alone selected for this special but important use?

Baptizo is found *eighty* times in the New Testa-

---

a Essay on Baptism, p.51. Bib. Reposit., 1833, p.298. *b* Socolia Matt. iii: 6. *c* Inst. loc. 19, quest. 11. *d* Chris. Dictionary. *e* Critica Sacra. *f* Disp. Bap., dis. 1. *g* Com. on Matt. iii: 6. *h* Thans. Four Gospels. Note on Matt. iii: 11.

ment. In nearly seventy it is used to designate the ordinance of baptism. Dr. Carson, Prof. Stuart and others have abundantly proven that this word means to *dip*, plunge or immerse, and that it means nothing else. Over 18 years ago (1888) an offer from a responsible party, was published in the *Western Recorder* and copied in other papers, offering a reward of a thousand dollars to any one who would produce a single passage from the Greek of either the classic or the New Testament period where the Greek word *baptizo* means either sprinkle or pour. While the offer caused some bluster, no such passage has been produced or can be produced. That offer still stands. It is not that passages have been produced on which opinions differed as to the meaning of *baptizo*. In that case professors of Greek in universities, to be agreed upon, would be asked simply to translate the given passage, without note or comment, the matter to be settled by their translation. If the Greek word *baptizo* means sprinkle or pour at all, it must have that meaning *somewhere* in the Greek. Since it has no such meaning *anywhere*, it has no such meaning at all. Our Saviour, in leaving a command universally binding on His disciples, meant to express it so simply, so plainly and so positively, that none could misunderstand it. Therefore, this word was used, which means strictly and positively, just what He intended and nothing else.

Bapto is found *three* times in the New Testament, and this also means *dip*, but is never applied to baptism. Why not? Because it has other meanings also, as well as to dip, and with this word the ordinance might easily have been misunderstood.

Louo is found six times, and means to *wash*. to wash the whole body; to bathe. If, as some say, baptisms means to wash, here was just the word to express it. But this word is never applied to the ordinance, because washing was not meant.

Nipto means, in like manner, to *wash*, but to wash the extremities, as the face, hands, or feet, as distinguished from bathing the whole body This word is found *seventeen times*, but is never applied to baptism. Why not, if a little water applied to the face may be baptism?

Rantizo means to *sprinkle*, and is found in the New Testament *four* times. This would have been the very word used to designate baptism if, as some say, that ordinance is properly performed by sprinkling. But this word is in no instance so used. Why not? Because sprinkling is not baptism.

Keo means to *pour*, and is found many time in its various combinations, but is never applied to baptism. If baptism is pouring water on the candidate, why was not this word sometimes used to express it?

Katharizo means to *purify*, to cleanse, and is found *thirty* times, but never applied to the ordinance of baptism. If, as some say, the ordinance means to purify, this word would have expressed it.

Let it be asked again, Why did Christ and His

apostles, of all the words in the Greek language, select, always and only, that *one* which means, strictly and positively, *dipping* or *immersion*, and nothing else, to designate the ordinance which He commanded and they administered? Simply and only because baptism meant *dipping* or immersing, and nothing else.

THE END.

WHAT THE SCHOLARS SAY.

PRESBYTERIAN.

John Calvin: "The very word *baptize* signifies to immerse; and it is certain that immersion was the practice of the ancient church." Institutes Book IV, chap. IV.

Thomas Chalmers: "The original meaning of the word baptism is immersion. we doubt not that the prevalent style of the administration in the apostles' days was by an actual submerging of the whole body under water." Com. on Romans vi. 4.

Dr. Philip Schaff, on Col. ii. 12: "The passage shows that immersion was the mode in the apostle's mind."

METHODIST.

John Wesley. Notes on New Testament, on Rom. vi. 4: "*We are buried with him*, alluding to the ancient manner of baptizing by immersion."

Adam Clarke. Com. on New Testament, on Col. ii. 12: "*Buried with him in baptism*; alluding to the immersion practiced in the case of *adults*; wherein the person appeared to be buried under the water, as Christ was buried in the heart of the earth."

George Whitfield in 18th sermon, p. 297: "It is certain that in the words of our text, Rom. vi. 3, 4, there is an allusion to the *manner* of baptizing, which was by *immersion* which is what our church allows," etc.

EPISCOPALIAN.

Bishop Lightfoot, Commentary on Colossians, p. 182: "Baptism is the grave of the old man, and the birth of the new. As he sinks beneath the baptismal waters, the believer buries there all his corrupt affections and past sins; as he emerges thence, he rises regenerate, quickened to new hopes and a new life. ... Thus baptism is an image of his participation both in the death and in the resurrection of Christ."

Dean Stanley in Hist. Eastern Ch., p. 117: "There can be no question that the original form of baptism— the very meaning of the word—was complete immersion in the deep baptismal waters."

Bishop Smith, of Kentucky: "Immersion was not only universal six or eight hundred years ago, but it was *primitive* and *apostolic*, no case of baptism standing on record by any other mode, for the first three hundred years, except a few cases of those baptized clinically, lying in bed. If any one practice of the early church is clearly established it is immersion."—*Kendrick on Baptism*, p. 150.

LUTHERAN.

Martin Luther: "For to *baptize* in Greek is to *dip*, and *baptizing* is *dipping*. Being moved by this reason, I would have those who are to be baptized to be *altogether dipped into the water*, as the word doth express, and as the mystery doth signify."—Works, Wittem Ed., Vol. II., p. 79.

Mosheim. Eccl. Hist., Vol. 17 p. 129, speaking of baptism in the 1st century, says: "The sacrament of baptism was administered in this century, without the assemblies, in places appointed and prepared for that purpose, and was performed by immersion of the whole body in the baptismal font."

Neander. Hist. Chn. Rel., Vol I., p. 310, says of baptism in the first three centuries: "In respect to the form of baptism, it was in conformity with the original institution and the original import of the symbol, performed by immersion, as a sign of entire baptism into the Holy Spirit, of being entirely penetrated by the same."

ROMAN CATHOLIC.

Donay Bible. Haydock's Notes. Endorsed by the Pope, says on Matt. iii. 6: "*Baptized.* The word baptism signifies a washing, particularly when it is done *immersion,* or by *dipping* or *plunging* a thing under water, which was formerly the ordinary way of administering the sacrament of baptism. But the church, which cannot change the least article of the Christian faith, is not so tied up in matters of discipline and ceremonies. Not only the Catholic Church, but also the pretended reform churches, have altered this primitive custom in giving the sacrament of baptism, and now allow of baptism by pouring or sprinkling water upon the person baptized; nay, some of their ministers do it nowadays, by filliping a wet finger or thumb over the child's head, or by shaking a wet finger or two over the child, which it is hard enough to call a baptizing in any sense."

Cardinal Gibbons: "For several centuries after the establishment of Christianity, baptism was usually conferred by immersion; but since the twelfth century the practice, of baptizing by affusion has prevailed in the Catholic Church, as this manner is attended with less inconvenience, than baptism by immersion." *Faith of Our Fathers*, p. 275.

These are, but samples. Hundreds of similar testimonies from the best scholars of all denominations can easily be cited. If it is not certain that the, baptism of the New Testament was immersion, then nothing in history is certain.